DICTIONARY OF ACCOUNTING

This is a quick reference to nearly 2,000 accounting terms most frequently encountered by laymen and professionals. Each entry, set off in bold type for easy identification, is defined in clear, nontechnical language for readers not familiar with accounting terminology. The encyclopedic number of entries as well as the completeness of the definitions make this a useful work for professionals who occasionally need to refer to a less-frequently used word.

DICTIONARY OF
ACCOUNTING

David L. Scott
Valdosta State College

George Fiebelkorn
Valdosta State College

A HELIX BOOK

ROWMAN & ALLANHELD
Totowa, New Jersey

ROWMAN & ALLANHELD

Published in the United States of America in 1985
by Rowman & Allanheld, Publishers
(A division of Littlefield, Adams & Company)
81 Adams Drive, Totowa, New Jersey 07512

Copyright © 1985 by Rowman & Allanheld, Publishers

Library of Congress Cataloging in Publication Data

Scott, David Logan, 1942-
   Dictionary of accounting.

   (A Helix book)
   1. Accounting—Dictionaries. I. Fiebelkorn, George.
II. Title.
HF5621.S4   1985   657'.03'21   84-27619
ISBN 0-8226-0384-5 (pbk.)
ISBN 0-86598-164-7 (cl.)

84 85 86 / 10 9 8 7 6 5 4 3 2 1

Printed in the United States of America

DICTIONARY OF ACCOUNTING

A

AAA. See **American Accounting Association.**
abandonment. See **retirement.**
abatement. A partial or complete cancellation of a tax levy, special assessment, or service charge imposed by a governmental unit.
ABC method. An inventory control technique in which inventory items are assigned to classifications (a, b, and c) based upon their value or importance. Additional care is taken in controlling the more significant classifications.
abnormal spoilage. Product loss in the production process which is not expected to occur under efficient operating conditions.
abnormal waste. See **abnormal spoilage.**
absolute priority. The right of senior creditors or stockholders to receive full payment prior to any payments to holders of junior securities.
absorption costing. The method of product costing where fixed manufacturing overhead is allocated to units of product and included in the inventoriable or product cost. Contrast with **variable** or **direct costing.**
Accelerated Cost Recovery System. An arbitrary means of spreading the cost of tangible property over a statutory period of 3, 5, 10, or 15 years depending upon the type of

1

property. Salvage value is ignored and the cost recovery method and periods are the same for both new and used equipment. This approach to depreciation was established by the Economic Recovery Tax Act (ERTA) of 1981.

accelerated depreciation. Any of a number of depreciation methods in which more of the cost of a long-lived asset is allocated to and recognized as an expense in the earlier years of the asset's economic life than in later years. See also **declining balance depreciation, double declining balance depreciation,** and **sum-of-the-years'-digits depreciation.**

acceleration clause. A provision of a bond indenture which requires, in the event of default, that unpaid interest and remaining principal be paid within a short time.

acceptance sampling. A special form of attribute sampling in which an auditor can state, with a given level of confidence, that the error rate associated with the area being studied is below a previously specified tolerable error limit.

accommodation endorsement. A written agreement made by an individual to enable a second party to have a note payable accepted by a creditor.

account. 1) The record of the increases, decreases, and balances of an asset, liability, capital stock, revenue, or expense. 2) A page in the ledger containing information about an item that appears on the balance sheet or income statement.

accountancy. The activities, e.g., practice, teaching, and research comprising accounting.

accountant. An individual trained by way of education or experience in the subject of accounting and its various forms.

accountant's legal liability. The potential obligations that accrue to an accountant as a result of being charged with the failure to possess the generally accepted standards of competence and care as developed within the accounting profession, common law, and the

Federal Securities Acts of 1933 and 1934.

account form. The form of the balance sheet in which the assets are shown on the left side of the statement and the liabilities and owners' equity on the right side. Contrast with **report form.**

accounting changes. See **change in accounting estimate** and **change in accounting principles.**

accounting cycle. The sequence of steps associated with taking an economic event or transaction from its occurrence to its ultimate inclusion in the financial statements.

accounting information system. The structure of methods and procedures which records and reports information on the financial position, operations, and other activities of an organization for use in decision making by management and external users of the firm's financial information.

accounting interpretations. See **interpretations.**

accounting period. See **fiscal period.**

accounting principles. Fundamental guidelines which serve as the basis for the preparation of financial statements.

Accounting Principles Board. A committee of the American Institute of Certified Public Accountants which, prior to the establishment of the Financial Accounting Standards Board in 1973, established generally accepted accounting standards.

accounting procedure. The methods or techniques which discover, record, or summarize financial information in the production of financial statements.

Accounting Research Bulletins. The 51 (1939-1959) publications of the AICPA's Committee on Accounting Procedure which dealt with a variety of then timely accounting problems.

accounting theory. The broad conceptual framework of basic principles, procedures, methods, and techniques, that guide the practice of

3

accounting.

accounts payable. Amounts owed on open account for goods or services received by an organization.

accounts receivable. Amounts due on open account from other organizations as a result of providing goods or services.

accounts receivable turnover. See **ratios.**

accrual accounting. See **accrual basis.**

accrual basis. The method of accounting under which revenues are recognized when earned and expenses are recognized when they result in obligations for benefits received regardless of the receipt or payment of cash. Contrast with **cash basis.**

accruals. Items of revenue, expenses, receivables or payables that are recorded as a result of the use of the accrual basis of accounting.

accrue. The procedure which records revenues when earned and expenses when they are incurred in association with the receipt of benefits. This procedure does not consider the timing of cash receipts or payments.

accrued asset. An asset that arises as the result of an accrued revenue.

accrued expense. An expense incurred and therefore recorded in an accounting period but which will not be paid until a subsequent accounting period. See also **accruals** and **accrue.**

accrued income. See **accrued revenue.**

accrued liability. An obligation that arises as the result of an accrued expense, e.g., wages payable.

accrued revenue. A revenue earned and therefore recorded in an accounting period but which will not be collected in cash until a subsequent accounting period. See also **accruals** and **accrue.**

accumulated depreciation. A contra account to depreciable plant and equipment which reflects all past depreciation recorded on these assets.

accumulated earnings tax. An additional tax

assessed on that portion of a corporation's accumulated taxable income which exceeds an amount established by formula. The purpose is to discourage the unnecessary retention of earnings that could be paid out as taxable dividends.

acid test. See **ratios.**

acquisition adjustment. In governmental accounting, the amount paid for a utility plant beyond its original cost less depreciation. Similar to goodwill in nonmonopolistic enterprises.

ACRS. See **accelerated cost recovery system.**

activity base. The production activity that is used to relate manufacturing overhead to units of production. Frequently used bases include direct labor dollars, direct labor hours, and machine hours.

activity ratio. A type of financial ratio that measures how intensively a firm uses various assets. Examples are asset turnover, inventory turnover, and average collection period.

actual costs. Costs determined on the basis of amounts actually incurred.

actuarial gains and losses. In accounting for pension costs, the gains/losses resulting from actual occurrences such as interest rates, or employee turnover being different from those assumed by the actuary in predicting the pension costs for a period.

additional paid-in capital. See **contributed capital in excess of par** or **stated value.**

adjusted basis. In tax accounting, the cost or other beginning investment in property reduced by depreciation and increased by capital improvements. Essentially the same concept as **book value** in financial accounting.

adjusted gross income. On an individual tax return, gross income less certain deductions associated with the production of income. It is used as a basis in determining the amounts deductible for such items as charitable contributions and medical expenses.

adjusting entry. A journal entry necessary under the accrual basis of accounting to update revenue, expense, asset, liability and stockholders' accounts for a transaction that should be recognized even though cash has not been received or paid. See also **accruals** and **accrue.**

administrative expense. A classification of expense based on the function of general expenditures necessary to operate the business as opposed to more specific functions such as selling or manufacturing.

ADR. See **Asset Depreciation Range.**

ad valorem. In governmental accounting, a basis for levying taxes in proportion to asset value. Especially used with real property.

adverse opinion. An opinion by an auditor (Certified Public Accountant) that the financial statements for an entity are not fairly presented in accordance with generally accepted accounting principles.

affiliate. An organization formally related to another by common management or ownership.

after-acquired property clause. A bond indenture provision that property acquired in the future will serve as additional collateral for the issue.

agency. A relationship where one person has the authority to act for another subject to their control.

agency fund. In governmental accounting, a fund made up of resources received and held by the governmental unit as an agent for another segment of government. For example, taxes collected and held by a municipality for a school district.

aging of accounts. A measure of the length of time accounts receivable have been outstanding. An aging schedule is useful in evaluating a firm's credit and collection policies.

AICPA. See **American Institute of Certified Public Accountants.**

AIS. See **accounting information system.**

all financial resources. See **total financial resources.**

allocation. Method of assigning costs or revenue to segments of an entity according to some reasonable measure of use such as benefit received.

allowance account. A contra account in which accumulated amounts, when netted with the parent account, result in a valuation adjustment so as to reflect a more realistic book value. An example is allowance for doubtful accounts which results in the accounts receivable account being reduced by the amount of the expected uncollectibles.

allowance for doubtful accounts. A contra account to accounts receivable showing the estimated amount of accounts receivable that will ultimately be uncollectible.

American Accounting Association. An organization, composed mostly of accounting educators, for promoting research and education in accounting.

American Institute of Certified Public Accountants. The oldest and largest national organization for CPAs. This group prepares and grades the CPA exam for state licensing bodies and its technical committees prepare pronouncements concerning accounting and auditing.

amortization. The gradual reduction, redemption, or liquidation of the balance in an account according to a specified predetermined table or schedule of dates and amounts. Generally used in conjunction with intangibles and liabilities.

amortize. to write off the cost of an asset over a specific number of time periods.

amount realized. In tax accounting, the sum of money plus the fair market value of other property or services received upon the sale or exchange of property. Determining the amount realized is the initial step in calculating the gain or loss on a transaction.

7

analytical review. A type of substantive test used in auditing to study and compare relationships among data. For example, an auditor calculates a ratio and compares it to some predetermined criterion. The auditor would then further investigate any ratio which seemed to be inconsistent with the established criteria.

annual percentage rate. Effective annual rate of interest on a credit arrangement.

annual report. The formal and complete report to shareholders and creditors of an organization of the past year's financial activities as audited by a CPA.

annuity. A series of equal periodic payments made at regular intervals.

annuity due. A series of equal periodic payments in which the payments are made at the beginning of each period. Contrast with an **ordinary annuity.**

annuity method of depreciation. Any of several methods of determining the periodic depreciation expense that results in more of the original costs being recognized in the later periods of the asset's life than in the earlier periods. This method, also known as **compound interest method,** is not found in practice, and is not considered a generally accepted accounting practice because the recognition of more expense in later years is not considered rational and systematic, i.e., logical.

antidilution provision. An agreement applying to convertible securities that, in the event a firm increases the number of shares of stock without a corresponding increase in assets or earning power (e.x., stock split, stock dividend, sale of new stock priced under market), the relative position of holders will be left unchanged. This is accomplished by altering the terms of conversion.

APB. See **Accounting Principles Board.**

APB opinions. Pronouncements of the Accounting

Principles Board which addressed and provided guidelines as to how controversial matters concerning the reporting of certain financial transactions were to be handled.

applied overhead. Manufacturing factory overhead that is allocated to products or services by means of some predetermined rate based on a budgeted amount of overhead.

appraisal surplus. See **unrealized increment.**

appreciation. An increase in value of an asset.

appropriated surplus. See **appropriation of retained earnings.**

appropriation. In governmental accounting, an authorization granted by a legislative body to incur liabilities for specific purposes set forth in the legislative act which established the appropriation. These are usually limited as to the amount and the time when they may be expended. See also **appropriation of retained earnings.**

appropriation of retained earnings. A reclassification of retained earnings in order to disclose that management does not intend to distribute assets up to the amount of the appropriation as a dividend because these assets are needed by the corporation for some specified purpose.

APR. See **Annual Percentage Rate.**

ARB. See **Accounting Research Bulletins.**

arrears. Past dividends of cumulative preferred stock that have not been paid. These dividends plus the current dividends on the cumulative preferred must be paid before common shareholders may receive a dividend.

articles of incorporation. The document filed with state authorities in applying for incorporation.

assessable stock. Capital stock sold originally at a price below par value and subject to a call for payment of the difference between sales price and par value.

assessed value. The value assigned property by a governmental body for the purpose of taxation.

asset. Resources which have current and future value.

asset depreciation range. An Internal Revenue Service schedule of upper and lower asset lives over which an asset may be depreciated for income tax purposes without further justification.

asset-linked bonds. See **commodity-backed bonds.**

asset turnover. A financial ratio which measures the extent to which assets are utilized. It is calculated by dividing average dollar amount of assets into annual sales.

assignment. Transferring title of a debtor firm's assets to a trustee who liquidates the assets for the benefit of the firm's creditors. This is an alternative to a formal bankruptcy proceeding through the courts.

assignment of accounts receivable. Borrowing cash from a lender by issuing a promissory note which contains a provision establishing certain accounts receivable as collateral.

association. An organization which clearly possesses corporate attributes and is treated as a corporation for Federal tax purposes even though it may not qualify as such under applicable state law. Attributes include: centralized management, continuity of existence, free transferability of interests, and limited liability.

attainable standards. Standards used in standard costing that can be expected to be reached given a reasonable amount of effort.

attest function. The process of independent review of an entity's financial statements by an auditor, i.e., certified public accountant, accompanied by an opinion as to the fairness of presentation.

attribute sampling. See **sampling.**

attribution. The situation in which Federal tax laws assign the ownership interest of one taxpayer to another taxpayer. The rule is applied when the relationship between the taxpayers is so close that there is essentially only one economic interest as, for example, with a parent and child.

audit. The examination, analysis, and evaluation by internal or external auditors of a process, procedure, or representation of an entity. Specific types of audits include:

financial audit. An audit whose purpose is to express an opinion by a CPA on the fairness with which financial statements of an organization are prepared in conformity with generally accepted accounting principles.

compliance audit. An audit whose purpose is to evaluate an entity's compliance with a defined set of requirements.

internal audit. An audit conducted by employees of the entity. This type of audit is generally either of the compliance or operational type.

operational audit. An audit whose purpose is to evaluate the effectiveness and efficiency of some segment of an organization in achieving its goals within the organization.

audit committee. A committee of the board of directors that is responsible for the financial reporting function including the selection of outside auditors, supervision of internal auditors, and review of the entity's internal controls.

audited statements. Financial statements which have been audited by a CPA.

audit evidence. Information that is acceptable and utilized by an auditor in rendering an opinion.

auditor. An individual who conducts audits.

audit procedures. The methods of applying auditing techniques to a particular activity or transaction.

audit trail. The link established between each transaction and its ultimate disposition that permits a means of tracing from source document to financial statement, and vice versa.

auditing. The objective and systematic method of obtaining and evaluating evidence concerning an activity in order to render an opinion concerning the activity.

audit program. The schedule of techniques, procedures, and methods necessary to accomplish the goals of an audit.

audit report. The opinion of an auditor concerning the finding and evaluation of an audit.

audit trail. The record of documented evidence in support of the accounting system. So named because the documentation leaves an unbroken "trail" as to what has occurred.

authority. In governmental accounting, a public agency established to perform a specific function or restricted group of related activities. Authorities may or may not be completely independent of other governmental units and may have taxing powers but are usually financed through service charges, tolls, etc.

authorized stock. The maximum number of shares of stock that may be issued by a corporation under its incorporation within the laws of the state that issues its articles of incorporation.

autonomy. The amount of freedom permitted a manager in the making of decisions.

average collection period. See **ratios.**

average cost. Method of assigning cost to individual items in a group based on dividing the total cost of the group by the number of items in the group.

avoidable costs. Costs associated with a particular operation that will not continue to be incurred if the operation is changed or stopped.

B

back order. An order for goods or services that has not yet been delivered. Normally, back orders are the result of merchandise being out of stock.

bad debt expense. An expense account that reflects the estimated uncollectible credit sales for the period of time covered by the income statement.

bad debts. Accounts or notes receivable that are determined, after reasonable efforts at collection, to be uncollectible.

balance. 1) The book value of an asset. 2) For an account, the difference between debits and credits. 3) To verify that the debits and credits to an account are accurate.

balance sheet. The financial statement which presents the assets, liabilities, and owners' equity of an entity as of a specific date.

balloon payment. The final payment on a loan that is considerably larger than the preceding payments.

banker's acceptance. A short-term promissory note, written on and endorsed by a bank, to pay a specific sum on a certain date. Used in both domestic and international trade when the customer's credit has not been established with the seller.

bank overdraft. A liability resulting from

writing checks totaling more than the balance on deposit.

bank reconciliation. The analysis of differences between the balance reported by the bank for a checking account and the amount shown on the depositor's books.

bank statement. The periodic statement prepared by a bank and sent to a depositor showing the details of activity within the account for the period. Especially applies to checking accounts in which cancelled checks are normally returned to the issuer together with a record of bank charges and credits.

bankruptcy. The state of insolvency where assets of the debtor are turned over to a receiver or trustee for administration.

Bankruptcy Reform Act of 1978. Legislation which streamlined bankruptcy cases to allow them to be settled more quickly. The major sections of the Act, Chapters 7 and 11, allow for liquidations and reorganizations, respectively.

bargain purchase option. A lease option permitting the lessee to purchase the leased property at such a favorable price that the purchase is fairly certain to occur.

bargain renewal option. A lease provision which allows the lessee to continue the lease for an amount that is significantly less than the expected fair rental of the property at the date the option becomes exercisable.

barter. Exchanging goods and services directly without the use of a medium of exchange.

base period. The period of time that serves as a comparison standard. For example, the base period for the consumer price index is 1967.

base stock. The minimum level of inventory considered to be permanent in the base stock method of costing inventory.

base stock method. The method of determining the cost of inventory in which a base stock or minimum level is valued at a normal price and any additional quantity is valued on a last-in, first-out basis.

basing point. The location from which a seller calculates shipping charges in determining delivered price. The basing point is not necessarily the point from which a good is shipped.

basis. The value assigned to an asset for federal tax purposes. When assets are acquired by purchase, the basis is cost. Special rules apply to property acquired by other means.

basket purchase. The acquisition of multiple assets for one lump sum price. A portion of the aggregate cost should be allocated to each of the assets.

bearer bond. A long-term debt security that is not registered to the owner but has title vested in the holder. Typically, interest payments are received upon presentation of coupons that are attached to the bond. Contrast with **registered bond.**

beginning balance. The balance in an account at the start of a fiscal period.

beginning inventory. The dollar balance of the inventory account at the start of an accounting period.

betterment. An addition or change made to a long-term asset which either prolongs its life or increases its efficiency. The costs of the betterment are added to the book value of the asset.

Big Eight. The eight largest public accounting firms in the United States. The Big Eight is comprised of Arthur Anderson & Co., Arthur Young & Co., Coopers & Lybrand, Deloitte, Haskins & Sells, Ernst & Whinney, Peat, Mitchell & Co., Price Waterhouse & Co., and Touche Ross & Co.

bill. A written invoice of charges.

bill of exchange. A draft used primarily in international trade which orders a third party to pay a specific sum of money to the drawer.

bill of lading. A document issued to a shipper by a common carrier showing that the latter has received the goods and they are in transit.

bill of materials. A list of the direct materials required for the efficient production of a given volume of output.

blanket mortgage bond. A bond in which all real assets of the firm act as security.

blue sky laws. State laws that attempt to prevent fraud in the issuance and sale of securities by requiring their registration. So called because they attempt to prevent investors from being sold a "piece of the sky."

bond. A security that obligates the issuer to pay, over an extended time, periodic interest at a specified rate on the face value plus pay the face value on a designated maturity date. Corporate bonds are generally understood to have a maturity value (face value) of $1,000 unless stated otherwise. Interest payments are usually made semiannually but the interest rate is typically expressed on an annual basis.

bond discount. The amount by which the proceeds of a bond offering are less than the face value. The discount is treated as an expense and amortized over the life of the bond issue.

bond indenture. The contract between the issuer and the bondholders setting forth the particulars concerning a bond issue.

bond premium. The amount by which the proceeds of a bond offering are more than the face value. The premium is treated as a reduction in interest expense income and amortized over the life of the bond issue.

bond rating. Investment quality judgments of publicly traded bonds by financial services such as Moody's and Standard & Poor's. A bond's rating has a strong influence upon the yield it must offer to attract investors.

bookkeeper. An individual who records transactions and prepares financial statements.

book value per share. The amount that could be expected to be distributed to each share of common stock if assets were liquidated at their balance sheet amounts. It is calculated by subtracting the par value of preferred stock (if any) from stockholders' equity and dividing the difference by the average number of shares of outstanding common stock.

boot. In tax accounting, any additional money or other property received in conjunction with an exchange of property that results in the recognition of a gain not to exceed the fair market value of the boot received.

breakeven analysis. An analytical technique for examining the relationships among a firm's sales, fixed costs, variable costs, and profits.

breakeven chart. A diagram that illustrates variable costs, fixed costs, total costs, and total revenues over a range of output.

breakeven point. The volume of sales at which total revenue equals total costs and profits are zero. Volume may be expressed in units or dollars.

bridging loan. A short-term loan designed to provide temporary funds until longer-term financing can be arranged.

budget. A financial plan showing estimates or goals in place of actual amounts for the items that appear on the financial statements. A budget serves as a guide for future operations and, once the operations are complete, as a standard for the evaluation of performance.

budget variance. See **variance.**

burden. See **manufacturing overhead.**

business combination. The joining of two or more companies to form a single entity for the conducting and reporting of business activities.

bylaws. The rules setting forth the method in which a corporation's functions are to be conducted. These rules cannot be in conflict with the articles of incorporation.

by-product. A secondary product associated with a manufacturing process that produces multiple products. The value of a by-product is normally small compared to the primary product(s). Also see **joint costs.**

17

C

CA. See **chartered accountant.**

call. Redeeming a security prior to maturity by forcing holders to sell at a specified price. Not all security issues are subject to call.

callable bond. A long-term debt security which the issuer has the right to reacquire at a predetermined price on specified dates in order to retire it prior to maturity.

call premium. The amount by which a security's call price exceeds its face value. The premium normally does not apply to purchases for sinking fund requirements.

call price. The price at which an issuer can repurchase its securities prior to maturity by forcing holders to sell. The call price normally declines over time and the price for sinking fund purposes is different than that for purposes of refunding.

call protection. A prohibition against calling a security issue for a specified period of years after the date of issue. This provision protects security holders during a period of declining interest rates.

call provision. An indenture provision that permits an issuer to repurchase a security prior to maturity by forcing security holders to sell at a specified price. Most bond and preferred stock issues are subject to call.

cancellable lease. A lease that may be cancelled by the lessee at any time. See also **lease.**

capacity variance. See **variance.**

capital. 1) Shareholders' equity (investment plus retained profits) of a business. 2) The long-term productive assets of a business.

capital addition. The addition, as opposed to the replacement of an old part, of a new part to an existing long-term productive asset such that the service capacity of the asset is increased. **capital asset.** 1) In tax accounting, any asset except those specifically excluded by the IRS Code. Major assets not classified as capital assets include inventory, trade accounts, notes receivable, and depreciable and real property used in a trade or business. 2) In financial accounting, any long-term productive asset.

capital budgeting. Measuring and evaluating the cash flows of long-term investment proposals for the purpose of allocating limited resources to the most desirable projects or segments of the business.

capital consumption allowance. See **depreciation.**

capital expenditure. An outlay for assets or improvements to assets that will benefit several time periods (years). The expenditure is recorded as an asset with portions being charged to current operations in periods in which the benefits are received.

capital gain. For tax purposes, the excess of proceeds over adjusted basis from the sale or exchange of a capital asset.

capital gains tax. See **capital gains treatment.**

capital gains treatment. A special method of calculating the income tax consequences for gains and losses realized on disposal of capital assets held by individuals for over six months. Currently (1985), only 40 percent of the gain is taxable.

capitalization of interest. The concept that the cost of certain long term assets should include the interest associated with and incurred during the construction period. Normally interest is not capitalized but expensed during the period incurred.

capitalization rate. The rate at which a series of future cash flows is discounted to calculate present value. The rate is higher when the flows are less certain.

capitalize. To record an expenditure that will yield benefits over several future periods as a long-term asset rather than as an expense.

capital lease. The type of lease in which the lessee, in substance, acquires an asset under conditions similar to an installment purchase. The lessee records the lease as an asset and a liability at the lower of: a) the present value of the total of the minimum lease payments during the lease term, or b) the fair market value of the leased asset at the inception of the lease.

capital leverage. A business's ability to generate a greater return from the use of borrowed funds than the cost of borrowing the funds. The excess accrues to the benefit of owners.

capital loss. For tax purposes, the excess of the adjusted basis over proceeds from the sale or exchange of a capital asset.

capital maintenance. The concept that before there can be income, revenues must be adequate to maintain the firm's current capacity to produce, e.g., inventory and long-term assets must be replaced as they are consumed.

capital market. A financial structure in which individuals, businesses, and governments exchange long-term debt and equity funds.

capital outlay. See **capital expenditure.**

capital projects. See **capital budgeting.**

capital rationing. See **capital budgeting.**

capital stock. See **common stock.**

capital structure. The composition of preferred stock, common stock, retained earnings, and long-term debt maintained by a firm in financing its assets.

capital surplus. An archaic term for contributed capital in excess of par or stated value.

carryback/carryforward. A provision in the Internal Revenue Code that permits certain items that cannot be fully utilized in a current tax year to be used in amending prior tax returns or recognized in future tax returns. An example is charitable contributions exceeding an amount established by formula in a given year that may be used as deductions in subsequent years.

carrying charge. The amount periodically added to a receivable to compensate the owner for interest and other expenses associated with holding the account.

carrying costs. Costs associated with having an item in inventory. For example, storage, insurance, and property taxes.

carrying value. See **book value.**

carryover. See **carryback/carryforward.**

CASB. See **Cost Accounting Standards Board.**

cash. Currency, coin, and bank account balances that are unrestricted in their use. Cash is a current asset.

cash basis. The method of keeping records in which revenues and expenses are recognized in the periods they are received and paid regardless of when they are earned or incurred. Contrast with **accrual basis.**

cashbook. A combined cash receipts and cash payments journal.

cash breakeven point. The volume of sales at which cash receipts equal cash expenses. The major noncash expense, depreciation, is not included in calculating the cash breakeven point.

cash budget. A schedule of expected cash receipts and expenses over a specified period of time. The primary purpose of maintaining a cash budget is to forecast when cash surpluses and deficits will occur.

cash cycle. The period which elapses between the time a firm expends cash to purchase materials and the time cash is collected when the goods associated with the materials are sold.

cash disbursements journal. A special journal used exclusively to record the disbursements of cash.

cash discount. A credit arrangement whereby a firm's customer is permitted to remit a fraction of the amount of an invoice if payment is made within a specified number of days. Cash discounts are offered to entice customers to pay their bills early.

cash discount period. The length of time between the date on an invoice and the last day on which a customer is able to obtain a cash discount. Credit terms of 2/10 net 30 offer a cash discount period of ten days.

cash dividend. See **dividends.**

cash equivalent. The monetary equivalent of noncash payments or receipts involved in a transaction. See also **payment in kind.**

cash flow. The net cash produced over a period of time. The flow may apply to a particular project or to an entire organization.

cash flow statement. See **change in financial position statement.**

cash forecast. A schedule of projected cash receipts and disbursements over a given period of time.

cash over/short account. An account reflecting the discrepancy between cash counted on a daily basis and cash register readings.

cash payments (disbursements) journal. See **journals.**

cash receipts and disbursements. See **change in financial position statement.**

cash receipts journal. See **journals.**

cash surrender value. An asset, usually reported under investments on the balance sheet, that represents the amount an insurance policyholder would receive upon cancellation of a life insurance policy.

casualty loss. In tax accounting, a loss due to some sudden, unusual, or unexpected event such as flood or fire.

CD. See **certificate of deposit.**

Certificate in Management Accounting. A professional designation awarded by the National Association of Accountants.

certificate of deposit. Receipt of short-term debt (with a specific maturity and interest rate) issued by a financial institution to a depositor. Negotiable certificates trade in a secondary market prior to maturity.

certificate of incorporation. See **articles of incorporation.**

certified check. A depositor's check with payment guaranteed by the bank on which the check is written. The guarantee is normally shown by an endorsement across the check's face.

Certified Internal Auditor. A professional designation awarded by the Institute of Internal Auditors.

Certified Public Accountant. A professional designation awarded by a state based on various statutory requirements and passage of the Uniform Certified Public Accountants Examination.

CFA. See chartered financial analyst.

change in accounting estimate. Revision of one or more estimates used in an accounting procedure. For example, changing the estimated number of years of economic value in calculating depreciation.

change in accounting principle. A change from one generally accepted accounting principle to another generally accepted accounting principle. For example, a change from sum-of-the-years-digits to straight line depreciation.

Chapter 11. A section of the Federal Bankruptcy Act of 1978 that provides for court-supervised reorganization of a firm in order to allow it to return to an improved financial condition.

Chapter 7. A section of the Federal Bankruptcy

Act of 1978 that provides for the liquidation of a firm that cannot reasonably be expected to return to a viable and profitable operating condition.

charge. 1) A debit to an account. 2) A sale on credit.

charge and discharge statement. The periodic report prepared by a fiduciary showing the receipt and disposition of resources placed in its care.

charitable contributions deduction. Gifts of property or money to certain qualifying organizations that are permitted in calculating taxable income. The amount of the deduction in any one tax year is normally limited to 50 percent of an individual taxpayer's adjusted gross income. The corporate limit is 5 percent of taxable income.

chartered accountant. A professional designation for accountants this is awarded by many present and former countries comprising the British Commonwealth. Similar to a certified public accountant in the U.S. in that the designation represents a level of education, experience, and knowledge.

chartered financial analyst. A professional designation for individuals who have met certain standards with respect to experience, conduct, and knowledge of financial analysis. The award is made by the Institute of Chartered Financial Analysts.

chart of accounts. A schedule of the accounts used by an organization.

chattel mortgage. A loan on real property other than real estate. Title is kept by the borrower but sale of the property is prohibited without the lender's consent.

check. A negotiable instrument that is a written order to a bank to pay, from the issuer's account, a specified amount to the holder.

check register. The book of original entry for all cash disbursements paid by check.

CIA. See certified internal auditor.

claim. A demand for payment.

classified common stock. Common stock issued by a company that has more than one class of common outstanding. Each classification is set apart according to its voting power and/or claim on earnings.

clean opinion. See **standard opinion.**

clean-up provision. A requirement of a lending institution that a borrower repay, or "clean up," its short-term debt at some point during the year. The purpose is to assure that the creditor is utilizing the funds for short-term purposes.

closed-end mortgage. A mortgage that prohibits the sale of additional bonds of equal priority from using the same property as collateral.

closely-held corporation. A corporation which is owned by a limited number of individuals with shares of stock that are not publicly traded.

closing. The finalizing of a sale or contract.

closing entries. Journal entries made at the end of an accounting period to transfer the net effect of revenue and expense items from the income statement to the owners' equity section of the balance sheet. This procedure also zeros out the revenue and expense accounts so that at the end of the following period they will reflect only the activities of that period.

closing the books. The process of clearing the revenue and expense accounts at the end of a period in order to start the next period with a zero balance.

cluster sample. See **sampling.**

CMA. See **Certificate in Management Accounting.**

Code. See **The Internal Revenue Code.**

co-insurance. A possible provision in a casualty insurance policy that requires the policyholder to insure property for at least a specified minimum percentage of its fair market value or share the loss proportionately with the insurance company.

collateral. Assets that are pledged by a borrower

as security for a loan. The creditor is entitled to these assets should the borrower fail to repay the loan.

collateral trust bond. A long-term debt security that is secured by other bonds or stock.

collection period. The period of time between when a product is sold and when cash is collected from the purchaser.

comaker loan. A loan signed by a party other than the borrower and who becomes responsible for payment in case the borrower defaults.

combined financial statements. See **consolidated financial statements.**

comfort letter. A statement by a CPA, given to the underwriter and legal counsel associated with a securities offering, that asserts the CPA has no information to indicate the issuing company's financial statements are false or misleading.

commercial paper. Short-term, negotiable, unsecured promissory notes of firms with a very high credit standing. Denominations are $100,000 or more and original maturities are 270 days or less.

commitment fee. A charge paid by a lender to ensure an access to credit.

committed costs. Fixed costs that result from acquiring items for which there is a long-term obligation.

commodity-backed bonds. A long-term debt security which is redeemable with a commodity such as gold, coal, or pork bellies, etc.

common costs. See **joint costs.**

common size financial statements. Financial statements that show the individual items in percentage form rather than dollars. This type of presentation is known as vertical analysis.

common stock. Shares of ownership in a corporation having voting rights and residual claims to profit distributions (dividends). When only one class of stock is present it is sometimes called capital stock. Also see **classified common stock.**

common stock equivalent. Any security, such as stock options, warrants as well as certain preferred stock and bonds, that may be exchanged for common stock. The characteristics of common stock equivalents, are so close to those of common stock that the security is considered to be essentially equal to common stock. This concept is used in determining the number of shares in calculating earnings per share.

comparability. The concept that financial statements should be prepared in such a manner that statements for several periods can be compared.

compensating balance. A minimum or average account balance which must be maintained at a financial institution. This may be required as part of a loan agreement or for the performance of certain designated services.

compilation. A service offered by a CPA that is essentially bookkeeping assistance.

complex capital structure. The situation where the ownership shares of a corporation are represented by more than one class of stock. The determinate is the requirement that a dual presentation (primary and fully diluted) of earnings per share be prepared.

compliance audit. See **audit.**

compliance tests. Examinations of the internal accounting control system made while conducting an audit in order to provide evidence as to whether controls prescribed by the system are being followed.

composite depreciation. A method of calculating periodic depreciation expense in which heterogenous assets are combined and the depreciation expense recognized is based on the cost of the group rather than on the cost of the individual assets.

compound entry. A journal entry with more than one debit or credit account.

compound interest. Interest that is calculated on the accumulated interest of preceeding periods as well as on the original principal that generated the interest.

compound interest method of depreciation. See **annuity method of depreciation.**

comptroller. See **controller.**

conglomerate merger. A combination of firms having unrelated product lines.

conscience money. Money received by an entity in payment for the previously undisclosed debts of an individual resulting from embezzlement, tax evasion, etc.

consent dividend. Retained earnings transferred to paid-in surplus where the stockholder is taxed as though he actually received a distribution when, in fact, he did not.

conservatism. The concept that when more than one acceptable alternative exist concerning the treatment of a transaction, the alternative having the least favorable effect on income or asset valuation should be chosen.

consignment. The transfer of the physical custody of an item to an entity that acts as an agent for the owner who retains legal title. This type of arrangement occurs so the agent can sell the item for the owner.

consistency. The concept that the same accounting procedures, techniques, and methods should be followed period after period so that the financial statements will be comparable.

consol. A perpetual bond (no maturity).

consolidated financial statements. The financial statements of a group of related companies composed of a parent company and one or more subsidiary companies. The statements are combined to provide a better representation of the economic reality of the financial activities of the association than would separate statements for the parent and each individual subsidiary.

consolidation. The combining of the accounts of a parent company and its subsidiary companies to produce consolidated financial statements. In this process, transactions between the

28

companies in the group are eliminated. A minority interest is shown if a portion of any subsidiary is not owned by the parent. See also **consolidated financial statement** and **minority interest.**

constant dollar accounting. The restating of the financial statements in dollars of equivalent purchasing power through the use of an appropriate index.

constructive dividend. A payment received by a stockholder that is deemed to be a dividend for tax purposes even though the benefit is not called a dividend. These attempts to avoid the double taxation associated with dividends include unreasonable compensation, excessive rent payments, and bargain purchase of corporation assets.

constructive ownership. The ownership of shares of stock for purposes of determining the percentage of ownership of a stockholder when the shares are actually held by certain other closely associated persons. Examples are parents, spouse, business partners, son/daughter, etc.

constructive right. Choosing not to receive income that is unreservedly subject to demand and could have been received. Constructively received income is taxable under a provision in the Internal Revenue Code.

contingent asset. An asset that may be obtained in the future if an event that was initiated in the past is successfully completed in the future, e.g., favorable lawsuit. Such assets should not be shown on the balance sheet, but may be disclosed in the footnotes.

contingent gain. A gain that may be realized in the future depending on the eventual outcome of an action started in the past. Such a gain should not be shown on the income statement. See also **contingent asset.**

contingent liability. A potential liability that may result in a future obligation if an event that was initiated in the past has an unfavorable outcome, e.g., adverse tax court decision. An estimated amount for the potential obligation should be included with the liabilities only if there is a significant probability that the event will have a detrimental outcome.

contingent loss. A loss that may materialize in the future depending upon the eventual outcome of some course of action begun in the past. Only those losses that are probable and reasonably measured are included on the income statement. See also **contingent liability.**

continuous budget. A twelve-month budget that is updated monthly by dropping the completed month and adding the corresponding month in the next year.

contra account. An account that is subtracted from another account in arriving at a value to use in the financial statements. The contra account is used in place of directly reducing the primary account and thereby continues to maintain the original information in the primary account. As an example, allowance for doubtful accounts is a contra account to accounts receivable.

contributed capital-in excess of par or stated value. An account on the balance sheet that represents the part of capital paid in by original stockholders which exceeds the par or stated value of the stock. For example, if a stock had a $10 par value and sold for $15, $5 would be contributed capital-in excess of par value.

contribution approach. The method of presenting revenue and expense information that emphasizes the relationship between variable costs and revenues. See also **contribution margin** and **contribution income statement.**

contribution income statement. An income statement which presents the determination of income in such a manner as to stress expenses as being either variable or fixed. The format of this type of statement is to subtract all variable expenses from sales revenue to obtain the contribution margin and then subtract all fixed costs to obtain income.

contribution margin. The portion of a firm's sales dollar that remains after variable costs are paid. The contribution margin indicates how each unit of output contributes to operating profits and covers fixed costs. It may be calculated on an aggregate or per-unit basis.

contributory pension plan. A pension plan in which the employee either pays for the cost of some of the benefits or makes payments to increase the benefits to be received.

control. The monitoring of a system or process by periodically comparing actual measurements with planned measurements and, if necessary, taking corrective action.

control account. An account that shows the total of a number of subsidiary accounts which is utilized to avoid cluttering the general ledger with individual accounts. For example, accounts receivable is a control account for the total of all individual credit customer accounts.

controllable cost. Cost that can be regulated, given a sufficient period of time and/or a given level of management.

controller. The top office in an organization responsible for internal control, cost accounting, financial accounting and reporting, and tax accounting. Sometimes termed comptroller.

conversion cost. The cost of transforming raw materials into finished products. Composed mainly of direct labor plus factory overhead.

conversion price. The amount of par value of a security which must be surrendered in order to obtain one share of common stock. Conversion price is calculated by dividing a convertible security's par value by the number of shares into which it may be exchanged.

conversion ratio. The number of shares of stock

for which a convertible security may be exchanged.

convertible security. A security, typically preferred stock or a bond, that can be exchanged for another type of security, generally common stock, at the option of the holder. The terms of conversion and period of time allowed for exchange are specified at the time of issue of the convertible security.

corporation. A legal entity created under state authority which operates separate from its owners. A corporation may incur liabilities, own assets, and pursue specific activities.

cost. The amount expended or owed for goods or services.

cost accounting. The field of accounting that is primarily concerned with the measurement, collection, and control of product costs. See also **managerial accounting.**

Cost Accounting Standards Board. The body established by Congress and charged with setting cost accounting rules for government contractors.

cost behavior. The indication of costs as they react to changes in levels of business activity. See also **variable costs** and **fixed costs.**

cost center. A responsibility center in which the supervisor is held accountable only for costs.

cost depletion. See **depletion.**

cost of capital. The annual cost of long-term liabilities and oqners' equity that is used to finance assets. A firm's overall cost of capital is a function of the cost of each component times the amount of that financing in the capital structure. New investments untaken that earn less that the cost of capital will tend to reduce the value of the firm.

cost of goods manufactured. The cost of products completed during a given period. Calculated as the sum of beginning work in process inventory plus direct material, direct labor, and factory overhead minus ending work in process inventory.

cost of goods sold. The total costs associated with an item sold that were incurred to acquire and prepare the item for sale.

cost plus fixed fee contract. Contracts in which revenue is cost plus a predetermined amount.

cost recovery method. A method of recognizing profit in installment sales or long contracts whereby profit is recognized only after collections exceed the costs of providing the item. Generally used when collectibility is uncertain.

cost-volume-profit analysis. See **breakeven analysis.**

coupon bond. See **bearer bond.**

coupon rate. Annual interest paid on a bond expressed as a percentage of par value. A bond with a face value of $1,000 and a 12 percent coupon rate would pay $120 in interest per year.

covenant. A provision in a loan agreement that is designed to protect the lender by placing a restriction on the borrower.

coverage ratios. Financial ratios that compare a firm's fixed obligations to its ability to service them.

CPA. See **certified public accountant.**

CPFF. See **cost plus fixed fee contract.**

credit. 1) The right to delay payment on a purchase. 2) An entry on the right side of an account which will result in a decrease in assets and an increase in liabilities or owners' equity.

credit against tax. A dollar for dollar reduction in tax liability that is allowed by the Internal Revenue Code because of certain activities. An example is the investment tax credit.

credit analysis. Evaluating the ability of an individual, firm, or other entity to meet its financial obligations.

credit instrument. A written document that permits delay in payment when purchasing an

33

item.

creditor. An entity to whom debts are owed.

creditors' committee. A group appointed to represent an organization's creditors in negotiating agreements with the debtor.

creditors' equity ratio. See **ratios.**

crossfoot. The process of adding horizontally all of the vertical totals in a multi-column array of figures in order to arrive at a grand total.

cum rights. With rights. A stock trades cum rights when the purchaser is entitled to receive rights that have been declared but not paid.

cum dividends. With dividends. A stock trades cum dividends when a new purchaser is entitled to receive a dividend that has been declared but not paid. Also see **ex-dividend date.**

cumulative dividends. See **cumulative preferred stock.**

cumulative preferred stock. A type of preferred stock in which payments to holders must be current prior to any distribution being made to holders of common stock. Most issues of preferred include a cumulative dividend feature.

cumulative voting. A method of voting for a firm's directors in which each share of stock entitles its holder to as many votes as the number of directors to be elected. Stockholders are permitted to accumulate votes and concentrate them to a limited number of directors. Cumulative voting allows minority interests to more easily gain representation on a board.

current assets. Cash or an asset reasonability expected to be converted, under normal operations, into cash within a year or operating cycle, whichever is longer. Examples are accounts receivable, marketable securities, and inventory.

current costs. Costs stated in terms of current market prices as opposed to historical costs.

current liability. An obligation that must be met within one year or one operating cycle and will require the use of a current asset or create another short-term obligation.

current ratio. See **ratios.**

current yield. The annual dollar amount of interest or dividends paid on a security divided by the price at which the security is currently trading.

D

data base. A non-redundant set of data that is organized so that it can be used for some purpose. For example, a catalogue of all items in inventory.

data base management system. A computer software program that has the ability to create, change, store, and retrieve data from a data base.

date of acquisition. The effective date on which an asset was acquired.

date of record. The date set by the board of directors on which security holders must be recorded on the organization's books in order to be entitled to receive dividends, rights, or voting privileges.

days sales in inventory. See **ratios**.

days sales outstanding. See **ratios**.

DBMS. See **data base management system**.

DDB. See **double declining balance**.

death taxes. A general term for any taxes due on an estate or the heirs of an estate upon the death of an individual. See also **estate tax** and **inheritance tax**.

debenture. A long-term debt security that is not secured by specific property but rather by the good name and earning power of the issuer. In case of liquidation, the owners of debentures become general creditors.

debit. 1) The left hand side of an account. 2) The amount shown on the left side of an account. 3) The process of placing an amount on the left side of an account. A debit to an asset account will generally increase the account total while a debit to a liability or owners' equity account will typically decrease the account balance.

debt. A short or long-term obligation that must ultimately be paid in cash, goods, or services. A liability.

debtor. One who has borrowed money or acquired goods or services from a lender (creditor) with an obligation to make payment in the future.

debt restructuring. A change in the type, form, or terms of a debt, e.g., replacement of short-term debt with long-term debt. A troubled debt restructuring occurs when a change is made in the original arrangement such that some advantage is granted by the lender to the borrower.

debt service. The dollar cost of meeting interest, principal, and sinking fund requirements over a given period of time.

debt to equity ratio. See **ratios.**

declaration date. The date on which a firm's directors establish the amount and time of the next dividend payment. At this point the amount of the dividend becomes a liability for the firm.

declining balance depreciation. A method of accelerated depreciation in which the periodic expense is calculated by multiplying a constant rate times an increasingly smaller book value or depreciation base of the asset. The periodic decline in the depreciation base is equal to the depreciation expense. See also **double declining balance depreciation.**

decommissioning cost. The expenses incurred in retiring a plant from service.

deduction. An expense permitted by a taxing authority in calculating income taxes. Normally used in reference to itemized deductions utilized in determining taxable income for federal income tax purposes. These include interest, charitable contributions, state and local taxes, medical expenses, and certain miscellaneous spending. See also **itemized deductions.**

deep discount bond. See **zero coupon bond.**

default. The failure to make a payment of money, goods, or services as required.

deferred charge. An expenditure considered to benefit the organization for several years in the future. The expenditure is capitalized and treated initially as an asset, but amortized as an expense during the periods of benefit. Essentially a long-term prepaid item. See also **prepaid expenses.**

deferred credit. 1) Long-term unearned revenue. Occurs when payment for goods or services is received, but performance is not required until some time in the future (greater than one year). Treated as a long-term liability and assigned to earned revenue as performance is made in the future. 2) A long-term liability arising from current recognition of an expense that will not be paid until some period in the future.

deferred income tax liability. An account showing the estimated amount of future federal income taxes associated with a transaction recognized for accounting purposes but not yet recognized under federal tax accounting. This is not an actual liability but an attempt to reconcile the difference between tax expense based on GAAP and taxes payable based on the Internal Revenue Code. See also **timing differences.**

deferred investment tax credit. The portion of an investment tax credit that is allocated over the useful life of the asset that brought about the credit. Deferring the credit is considered a more conservative approach than flowing it through in the period the asset is acquired. See also **flow-through accounting.**

deficit. A retained earnings account that has a debit balance instead of the typical credit balance. Arises from losses.

defined-benefit pension plan. A pension plan in which benefits are fixed and the employer's payments normally vary in order to provide for what has been specifically promised.

deflation. A general decrease in the price level of goods and services due to an increase in the purchasing power of the dollar.

demand deposit. A deposit in a financial institution that can be withdrawn without prior notice.

dependent. A qualifying individual who received over 50 percent of his or her support from the taxpayer. The dependent does not have to be a relative and the support does not necessarily have to be in the form of cash payments.

depletion. The process of spreading the original cost or basis of a natural resource to the periods in which the resource is extracted and sold. The two ways to determine depletion are cost and percentage (statutory).

   cost method. Each unit of the resource sold is assigned a pro rata share of the cost based on the total number of units expected to be recovered.

   percent method. A percentage, determined by the tax laws, is multiplied by the gross income from the resource to determine the periodic depletion expense.

depreciable assets. Those long-term assets subject to depreciation whose life and usefulness are limited because of such factors as obsolescence, wear and tear, and deterioration. Examples include buildings, equipment, and furniture. The most notable nondepreciable asset is land.

depreciation. The process of allocating the cost of a tangible asset to each period of its useful life in a systematic and rational manner. Depreciation occurs because plant and property have limited economic lives, and these assets future usefulness is eventually exhausted.

detailed audit. An examination of the accounting

record in which essentially all transactions are examined by an auditor. This procedure is undertaken when there is evidence of embezzlement. Normally, an audit involves an examination of only a sample of the transactions which are sufficient to allow an opinion concerning the overall financial operation.

development cost. See **research and development cost.**

differential cost. The amount by which total cost will change as the direct result of taking a specific course of action.

dilution. A reduction in the proportional ownership of one or more owners of a firm. Dilution may result from new shares of stock being sold or from convertible securities being exchanged for shares of common stock.

direct cost. Expenditures that can be easily and obviously traced to an organizational segment such as a product sales area, operating division, or other subset of a company. These expenditures are so closely related to the organizational segment that if the organizational segment ceases to exist the expenditures will no longer be required.

direct costing. The method of accounting for the products that are manufactured in which only variable costs, i.e., direct material, direct labor, and variable overhead, are considered product costs and assigned to inventory. Fixed costs are considered period costs. Contrast with **absorption costing.**

direct labor. Labor costs that are so closely related to the manufacturing of a product or providing of a service that, if the product was not manufactured or the service not provided, the labor wages need not be incurred. Contrast with **indirect labor.**

direct labor variance. See **variance.**

direct material. The costs of ingredients used in manufacturing a product that are so closely related to the product that, if the product was not manufactured, the cost of the ingredients need not be incurred. Contrast with **indirect material.**

direct material inventory. The supply of items classified as direct materials on hand as of the balance sheet date.

direct material variance. See **variance.**

director. A member of an organization's board of directors that guides the organization's course through setting policy and appointing operating officers.

disbursement. An outflow of cash from a business entity.

disclaimer. A statement by a certified public accountant that no opinion can be rendered on the financial statements of an entity because of lack of independence with respect to the reporting entity, insufficient evidence on which to have an opinion, or the outcome of significant matters is so uncertain that an opinion cannot be made.

discontinued operation. A line of business or class of customer that has been terminated. For example, a compact car division may be disposed of by an auto manufacturer.

discount. 1) The reduction in an original amount for some reason such as cash discount. 2) To reduce a future amount to its present value by using a discount rate.

discounted cash flow. The present value of all anticipated cash inflows net of cash outflows associated with a project. Projects that will provide a positive cash flow after being discounted by an appropriate discount rate are considered acceptable.

discounted present value. A method of evaluating projects in which the discounted future cash flows are compared to the outlay required. Projects with positive cash flows are acceptable.

discounting notes receivable. Securing cash through selling a note(s) receivable to a bank or other agent for an amount less than the proceeds (principal + interest) at maturity. When the note is transferred to the financial institution without qualification, the original holder remains liable if payment is not made. A note discounted with the endorsement "without recourse" relieves the original holder of future liability.

discount on bonds payable. The difference between the par value of bonds payable and a lower initial sales price. Bonds sell for less than par value when the market interest rate is greater than the interest rate stated on the bonds. The discount is gradually written off over the remaining life of the bonds by increasing (debiting) bond interest expense and crediting bond discount. At maturity there is no discount and the bonds are shown at their principal value.

discount rate. The rate of discount used to reduce a future amount to its present value.

discovery sampling. See **sampling.**

discretionary costs. Expenditures that, depending upon management policies, can either be incurred or forgone.

disposal value. See **residual value.**

dividend. Any distribution by a corporation out of earnings and profits of the taxable year or of accumulated earnings and profits. All dividends, except stock dividends, reduce the stockholders' equity in the corporation. Common types of dividends include:

cash dividend. A distribution, based on profitability, that is paid in cash. The dividend is declared by the board of directors at which time a current liability is created. Cash dividends are not declared and paid on treasury stock.

liability dividend. See **scrip dividend.**

liquidating dividend. A distribution of corporate assets to shareholders that represents a return of their original investment.

property dividend. A distribution based on

profit in which corporate assets other than cash are distributed to the shareholders.

scrip dividend. A distribution based on profit in which, instead of paying the dividend currently in cash, the corporation elects to make payment in cash at some future date and distributes, in the interim, a special form of note payable called scrip.

stock dividend. A distribution of additional shares of stock to shareholders which results in the capitalization of a part of retained earnings. No assets are distributed.

dividend payout ratio. The portion of earnings paid to common stockholders rather than retained in the business for reinvestment.

dividend reinvestment plan. An arrangement whereby a corporation's common stockholders may elect to have cash dividends automatically used to purchase additional shares of stock.

dividends in arrears. The amount of dividends on cumulative preferred stock associated with past periods that have not been declared, and thus, not paid. These arrearages plus the current dividend must be declared prior to any dividend declaration for common stock.

dividends payable. A current liability created by the declaration of dividends. Usually identified as being associated with either common or preferred stock. Also called cash dividend payable.

dividend yield. The annual cash dividend paid per share of stock divided by the stock's current market price.

dollar unit sampling. A sampling procedure that expresses in dollar amounts the conclusion that a particular attribute has been exceeded.

donated capital. Owners' equity that comes from the contribution of assets to the corporation in which an owners' interest is not given to the contributor.

double declining balance depreciation. A widely

used method of accelerated depreciation in which the constant rate used is twice the straight-line depreciation rate. For example, with straight-line depreciation an asset with a 10-year life would have a constant rate of decline in book value each year of 1/10 of original cost less salvage or a rate of 10%. Under the double declining method the constant rate would be 2 times 10% or 20% applying to the declining book value. See also **declining balance depreciation**, and **straight-line depreciation**.

double-entry bookkeeping. The system of keeping accounting records in which each transaction results in an entry in at least two accounts. For example, the sale of stock affects two accounts - cash and owners' equity.

draft. A written order requiring payment of a definite amount of money to the payee at a specific time or on demand.

E

early extinguishment of debt. The repurchase of long-term debt, usually bonds, prior to maturity, by the issuing firm. Gains/losses from this type of transaction are shown as extraordinary items on the income statement.

earned income. In tax accounting, income derived from personal services as opposed to income generated by property.

earned surplus. An archaic term for retained earnings.

earnings. Frequently used as a synonym for income or net income. Revenue minus expenses.

earnings and profits. In tax accounting, the income of a corporation that could be paid in dividends without a reduction in net worth. Nontaxable (e.g., interest on municipal securities) as well as taxable income is included although certain items used in calculating net income are excluded.

earnings per share. Earnings available to common shareholders divided by the average number of shares of common stock and common stock equivalents outstanding during the period. Also see **common stock equivalents, fully-diluted earnings per share,** and **primary earnings per share.**

earnings yield rate. See **ratios.**

economic life. The period of time over which an

asset is expected to provide efficient beneficial usefulness.

economic order quantity. The units of inventory that should be ordered at one time to minimize the total cost of ordering and carrying inventory.

EDP. Electronic data processing.

effective interest rate. See **yield rate.**

efficiency variance. See **variances.**

8-K. A report filed with the SEC by those corporations whose securities are traded on a national exchange or in the over-the-counter market, that states the details of any material event, such as a change in CPA firms. The form must be filed within ten days of the close of the month in which the event occurs.

embezzlement. The unauthorized and illegal taking of assets, especially money, that are in one's custody.

Employee Retirement Income Security Act of 1974. Legistration to ensure that employee retirement funds would be protected by setting standards for funding, vesting, eligibility, investment selection, and performance.

employee stock option plan. A policy established by a corporation to allow employees to acquire a predetermined number of shares of stock in the company under certain conditions.

encumbrance. In governmental accounting, contingent liabilities chargeable to an appropriation and, as a direct result, a portion of the appropriation is restricted for the anticipated expenditures. Encumbrances cease when paid or when the actual liability is recorded.

ending inventory. The inventory at the end of an accounting period.

engagement letter. A letter from a CPA to a client setting forth the specific tasks to be performed and the CPA's responsibilities concerning an audit.

engineered standards. Standard cost determined on the basis of engineered measurements rather

46

than estimates or extrapolation of historical data.

enterprise fund. In governmental accounting, a fund that provides goods or services to the public for a charge and usually with a profit motivation. Enterprise funds are accounted for in essentially the same way as profit-seeking businesses.

entity. Any separate identifiable concern such as a person, project, company, etc. See also **separate entity concept.**

entrepreneur. An individual who initiates and implements the various factors required to establish and operate a business.

EOQ. See **economic order quantity.**

EPS. See **earnings per share.**

equity. The claim by both creditors and owners against the assets of a company. The sources of the assets of a firm.

equity method. The method of accounting for significant investments in another corporation in which the investor's books reflect his share of the change in the owned company's net assets. Under this method, the original cost of the investment is increased, subsequent to purchase, to reflect a pro rata share of the owned company's reported earnings and decreased for dividends received and a pro rata share of the owned company's reported losses.

equivalent units. In theory, the number of units in a process costing system that could have been completed had all effort been directed toward completing units (no unfinished units at the end of the period). For example, 100 items, each 50 percent completed, could have been 50 units completed if all effort had been given to finishing units.

ERISA. See **Employee Retirement Income Security Act of 1974.**

ESOP. See **employee stock option plan.**

estate tax. A tax on the right to transfer property by death. This tax is levied on the estate and not on the heir to the property.

Contrast with **inheritance tax.**

estimated standards. Standard cost based on judgment and extrapolation of historical data rather than engineered measurements.

estimated tax payments. Quarterly payments that represent the estimated tax liability for income not subject to withholding.

estimated useful life. See **economic life.**

exception report. A document which reflects events that vary so much from the expected that management attention is required.

excess capacity. The condition whereby, for a long period of time, the ability to produce exceeds the requirement to produce. Contrast with **idle capacity.**

exchange rate. The rate at which one currency may be exchanged for another currency.

excise tax. A tax imposed upon a certain business or buying a specific product. Excise taxes may be levied against either a buyer or a seller.

ex-dividend date. The first day on which a stock trades that a buyer will not receive a dividend that has been declared. A stock's ex-dividend date is four business days prior to its record date. When stock is sold on or after the ex-dividend date, the seller will receive the dividend that has been declared.

executory costs. In a lease, those expenditures that are normally associated with ownership, such as insurance, taxes, and maintenance.

exempt income. Income items that are specifically exempt from inclusion in gross income for income tax purposes. Examples include interest on state and local debt, scholarships, and some employee benefits.

exemption. A deduction allowed to individual taxpayers for themselves and their dependents. An extra exemption is allowed individuals over 65 and an extra exemption is also allowed those who are blind.

exercise price. The dollar price which must be paid for a share of common stock when a warrant or right is exercised.

48

expected value. The weighted average of the amounts associated with an event or activity. Usually the outcomes associated with the events have been weighted by the probability of the likelihood of the event's occurrence.

expenditure. The amount of cash or other asset given, or liability incurred, in order to obtain an asset or service.

expense. The outflow of an asset in return for the inflow of revenue. An expense is shown as a deduction from revenue on the income statement.

experience gains and losses. See **actuarial gains and losses.**

exploration cost. The cost associated with the searching for natural resources, especially oil or gas.

ex-rights. Without rights. A stock trades ex-rights when the sellers, rather than the buyers, are entitled to receive rights that have been declared but not paid.

external auditor. A certified public accountant who performs an audit on a firm's financial statements. Also see **audit.**

external funds. Funds acquired outside the organization by selling stock or borrowing.

extra dividend. A payment to stockholders that is in addition to the regular dividend. An extra dividend is generally declared during an especially profitable period and may or may not be repeated.

extraordinary gain. See **extraordinary item.**

extraordinary item. An event or transaction that is both unusual in nature and infrequent in occurrence. For example, a lightening strike to a factory building. The gain or loss from such an event is shown net of taxes as a separate item on the income statement. Some transactions, such as the early extinguishment of debt, are required by the FASB to be reported as extraordinary even though they do not meet the unusual/infrequent test.

extraordinary loss. See **extraordinary item.**

extraordinary repair. A major overhaul of plant or equipment that is expected to extend its service life, useful life, or both.

F

face value. The nominal amount stated on a
security such as a bond or share of stock. In
the case of a bond, this amount is also termed
maturity value and in the case of stock, par
value.

factor. An individual (entity) buying receivables
at a discount.

factoring. Selling accounts receivable, without
recourse, at less than face value to another
party.

factory burden. See **manufacturing overhead.**

factory overhead. See **manufacturing overhead.**

fair market value. The sales price that would
prevail in an open market of a large number of
willing and able buyers and sellers.

FASB. See **Financial Accounting Standards Board.**

federal funds. Excess reserves depository
institutions have on deposit at Federal Reserve
Banks. Interest rates charged when
institutions loan these funds to other
institutions provide an indication of Federal
Reserve monetary policy.

fee. A charge for a service.

FICA. A wage and salary tax levied on employees
and employers to help finance the Federal
Insurance Contribution Act provisions of the
Social Security program.

fiduciary. One who is responsible for the assets

51

of another.

field warehouse. A storage area on a borrower's premises that is used to physically separate inventory being used as collateral for a loan. The area is controlled by a third party for the benefit of the lender.

FIFO. See **first-in, first-out.**

file. A collection of data associated with a particular subject within a data base.

financial accounting. The area of accounting concerned with the preparation and presentation of financial information to external users. Contrast with **managerial accounting.**

Financial Accounting Standards Board. The agency, established in 1973, that is responsible for setting generally accepted accounting principles.

financial audit. See **audit.**

financial forecasts. The presentation of futuristic information, especially the financial statements.

financial lease. See **leases.**

financial leverage. The extent to which a firm utilizes securities with a fixed return to finance assets. Increased financial leverage results in magnifying changes in operating income upon earnings per share.

financial position. The relationship of assets, liabilities, and owners' equity at a given point in time. The balance sheet data.

financial ratios. Ratios derived from comparisons of balance sheet items or comparisons of balance sheet items with income statement items. See also **ratios** and **ratio analysis.**

financial statement. A report stating certain financial information about an organization. Specifically, one of the following statements; balance sheet, income statement, retained earnings statement, or change in financial position statement.

financial structure. The mix of financing that is used to finance assets.

finished goods inventory. The items in a manufacturing firm that have been completed and are ready for sale.

first-in, first-out. An assumption as to the flow of costs in which the first items purchased or manufactured are presumed to be the first items sold.

fiscal period. Any period at the end of which an entity prepares financial statements.

Fiscal year. A period of 52 consecutive weeks plus one day or of 12 consecutive months.

fixed asset. An asset with an economic life greater than one year that is being held for its usefulness or revenue producing ability while being consumed as opposed to being held for resale or as an investment. Normally this term refers to land, plant, or equipment.

fixed charge coverage. See **ratios.**

fixed cost. Cost that, as it is incurred in relation to time or changes in the level of activity, does not change in total. Contrast with **variable cost.**

fixed overhead. Manufacturing overhead that is not expected to change when the level of production varies within a limited range known as the relevant range.

fixed overhead spending variance. See **variance.**

fixture. Any thing attached to a building that, while removable, is not really portable, e.g., carpeting.

flat. Priced without accrued interest.

flexible budget. A budget that shows the expected costs at various levels of activity.

float. The amount of funds that have been paid but not collected from the payee's bank. Float results from inefficiencies in the financial system.

floating rate bond. A long-term debt security on which the rate of interest is periodically adjusted according to a predetermined formula. In general, the rate more closely approximates short-term than long-term interest rates.

floating rate preferred. Preferred stock that

pays a dividend that is periodically adjusted according to a predetermined formula. The security normally trades at a price close to par with a current yield more closely approximating short-term than long-term interest rates.

flotation costs. Expenses incurred in issuing and marketing a new issue of securities.

flow chart. An abstract diagram of a process, system, or transaction using symbols and labels to show the flow of information and logic through the process.

flow-through accounting. Accounting for certain tax benefits, such as investment tax credits, by using them be reduce federal income taxes in the period in which they are secured. This is a relatively liberal method of treatment in that it increases current net income at the expense of future net income.

FMV. See **fair market value.**

FOB. See **free on board.**

FOB destination. Designation of the method of shipping goods where the seller pays the cost of transporting the goods to the buyer. Title to the goods transfers upon receipt by the purchaser.

FOB shipping point. Designation of the method of shipping goods where the buyer pays the cost of transporting the goods from point of shipment to destination. Title to the goods passes to the purchaser at point of shipment.

foot. To add a column of numbers. Contrast with **crossfoot.**

footnote. Narrative attached to and considered a part of the financial statements that explains items in the statements in greater detail.

forecasts. Financial statements prepared on a predicted or projected, as opposed to a historical, basis.

Foreign Corrupt Practices Act. A federal law that regulates the conduct of American businesses and businessmen. While the Act's primary intent is to prevent foreign bribery, it also requires all publicly held companies to maintain accurate records and an adequate system of internal control. The requirement for improved internal control also applies to companies not involved in international trade and is intended to prevent or detect undesirable activity.

foreign currency translation gains(losses). Gains and losses that come about as a result of operations in a different country. Such gains(losses) are not included in the determination of earnings but are shown net of taxes in the owners' equity section of the balance sheet.

foreign tax credit. A credit against domestic taxes for taxes paid to a foreign government.

forgery. Falsely making or altering a written instrument.

franchise. The right to conduct, for a specified period of time, a particular form of business in a particular area.

fraud. The intentional misrepresentation or deliberate concealment of a transaction for the purpose of willfully misleading someone. Contrast with **ordinary negligence** and **gross negligence.**

free on board. A specification in a sales contract indicating to what location the seller will assume the cost and risk of delivery.

freight-in. Shipping costs that must be paid by the purchaser on incoming goods.

freight-out. Shipping costs that must be paid by the seller on outgoing goods.

full costing. See **absorption costing.**

full disclosure. The concept that the financial statements should communicate in some manner all information that could influence a decision by users of the statements.

fully diluted earnings per share. A pro forma presentation of earnings per share that reflects the reduction that would have occurred if all contingent issuances of common stock that would in fact reduce earnings per share had been issued.

fully funded pension. A pension plan in which the assets of the pension are equal to or greater than the expected pension liability.

functional expense. The grouping of expenses into a general type of economic activity for which they are incurred. Examples are selling, manufacturing, and administrative.

fund. 1) An asset that represents cash, securities, or other assets being accumulated for a specific purpose such as the retirement of long-term debt. 2) A fiscal and accounting entity that reflects the economic activities of specific subdivisions of non-profit organizations, especially governments.

funded debt. Long-term debt of an organization.

funded pension plan. A pension plan in which the company deposits funds with an independent agency that is responsible for managing the fund and making payments to recipients as they are due.

funds. Cash or working capital.

funds-flow statement. See **change in financial position statement.**

furniture and fixtures. A long-term asset that includes the cost and accumulated depreciation for both furniture and fixtures.

FY. See **fiscal year.**

G

GAAP. See general accepted accounting principles.

GAAS. See Generally Accepted Auditing Standards.

gain. The excess of fair market value of economic goods received over the carrying value of the economic items given up in a transaction. As an example, the retirement of an $8,000 debt with a $5,000 payment results in a gain of $3,000.

GAO. See General Accounting Office.

General Accounting Office. A federal agency that was established by the U.S. Congress to monitor the performance and financial reports of other federal agencies.

general and administrative expenses. The classification of expenditures on the income statement that reflects operating expenses other than selling expenses and cost of goods sold.

general fund. In governmental accounting, a fiscal and accounting entity used to account for all transactions not recorded in another fund, that is, the ordinary operations of a governmental unit.

general journal. See journals.

general ledger. A book containing either a summary or detail of all transactions affecting the accounts of an entity, e.g., assets, liabilities, owners' equity, revenue, and expenses.

generally accepted accounting principles. The broad set of guidelines used to prepare financial statements for users external to the reporting entity. These principles are based primarily on FASB statements and APB Opinions but some, such as matching, are based on tradition and/or being widely advocated in accounting literature.

generally accepted auditing standards. The broad set of rules issued by the AICPA to guide the CPA in preparing for, conducting, and reporting the results of an audit of financial statements. Of the 10 broad guidelines, the first three deal with the auditor's qualifications, the next three are concerned with the performance of audit field work, and the last four address the reporting of the results of the audit. See also **statement on auditing procedure** and **statement on auditing standards.**

general obligation bonds. Municipal bonds that are pledged with the full faith and credit of the issuer.

general partner. A partner who has unlimited liability for the debts of a partnership.

general partnership. A partnership in which all of the partners are general partners and all are jointly and severally liable for the debts of the partnership.

going-concern. 1) A business whose financial situation is such that it is not expected to go out of business in the near future. 2) The assumption, in the absence of evidence to the contrary, that a business will continue to exist in the future.

going public. Selling shares of ownership in a corporation to the general public for the first time.

goods-in-process inventory. See **work-in-process inventory.**

goodwill. An unidentifiable characteristic of a business that results in the earning of superior returns on identifiable assets. While superior earning capabilities may be internally developed through activities such as advertising, only purchased goodwill may be recorded and reported in the financial records. Purchased goodwill is the excess of the purchase price of an entity over the fair market value of its identifiable net assets.

governmental accounting. 1) The procedures, principles, and concepts associated with accounting for municipal, state, and national governmental units. Differs from standard accounting in that this form incorporates budgetary amounts in the formal record keeping and imposes legal restrictions. 2) A general term for the techniques used in accounting for any not-for-profit organization.

gross income. In tax accounting, all income subject to federal income tax. Gross income does not include items specifically exempted from federal income tax such as interest on municipal bonds. Also used as a synonym for gross profit.

gross margin. See **gross profit.**

gross negligence. The failure to exercise due care through recklessness and the utter disregard of established standards. Contrast with **fraud** and **ordinary negligence.**

gross profit. The excess of net sales over cost of goods sold.

gross profit method. A means of determining ending inventory. The estimated gross profit ratio is multiplied by net sales to obtain gross profit. Gross profit is subtracted from net sales to obtain cost of goods sold. Cost of goods sold is subtracted from the total of the beginning inventory, plus net purchases (i.e., goods available for sale) to obtain an estimate of ending inventory.

gross profit ratio. The portion of sales that is left after a firm has paid for the cost of producing the goods. The ratio is calculated by subtracting the cost of goods sold from dollar amount of net sales and dividing the result by net sales.

gross sales. The total dollar amount of sales prior to accounting for returns and allowances.

group depreciation. A method of depreciation in which similar (homogeneous) assets having approximately the same useful lives are treated as essentially one unit. One depreciation rate is used for the group rather than for each asset. Used for such items as telephone poles and railroad ties.

guaranteed bond. A long-term debt security that is backed as to payment of interest and face value at maturity by an entity other than the issuer.

guaranteed residual value. The situation in a capital lease where the lessee insures the lessor that the leased asset will have a specified value at the end of the lease term.

H

hash total. A control measure to check for the possibility of errors. In the procedure a sum is made of a set of numbers entering the system, for example, the total of the check numbers. This sum is then compared with the total of the check numbers exiting the system. If the sums differ it is an indication that not all of the data was transmitted or processed.

head of household. In income tax accounting, an individual who provides more than half of the costs of maintaining a home for a dependent and/or an unmarried child.

hedge. Offsetting one position with another in order to eliminate potential losses. An example would be the purchase of inventory items prior to when they are required in order to offset potential price increases. Hedges often eliminate or reduce potential profits as well as potential losses.

hidden reserve. A situation that develops when the value of assets shown on the balance sheet is considerably below the true value. An example would be when assets depreciate at a slower rate than the accounting method assumes.

highlights. A summary of important financial and operating data.

historical cost. The amount originally recorded in a completed transaction that is unadjusted for subsequent changes in value. This amount is generally reflected in the financial statements because it is verifiable.

holders-of-record. Owners of a firm's securities who are listed on the firm's books on the record date.

holding company. A corporation that has controlling interest in the ownership of one or more other firms. Controlling interest does not necessarily require ownership of 51 percent of a firm's stock.

holding gains/losses. Unrealized gains or losses that result from having assets or liabilities during a period of changing prices.

holding period. The period of time property has been held. Especially important in determining for tax purposes whether a gain or loss on disposal receives long-term or short-term treatment.

horizontal analysis. The method of displaying current and past balance sheets of an entity side by side along with the dollar amount of increase(decrease) and respective percentage change.

human resource accounting. Systematically incorporating the value of human resources (employees) in an organization's accounting system. An example would be recognizing expenses involved in increasing human capital (recruiting) as similar to those used to purchase other long-term assets.

hurdle rate. The minimum rate of return that is acceptable on an investment.

hypothecate. To pledge an asset as collateral for a loan without delivering title or possession.

I

idle capacity. The amount of productive potential that is not being currently utilized.

idle capacity variance. See variance.

idle time. The period of time for which wage earners are paid but not productive due to machinery breakdowns, inadequate planning, or other similar reasons.

illiquid. 1) The condition of an asset when it is difficult to turn into cash without a significant discount in price. 2) The condition of a firm that has difficulty meeting its short-term obligations.

impairment of capital. The reduction in capital caused by losses or distributions.

impound. In governmental accounting, to withhold appropriations in order to limit authority to incur obligations.

imprest petty cash fund. A system of accounting for petty cash in which the balance remains constant unless the established amount for the fund is changed.

improvement. See betterment.

imputed interest. The interest or rate of return it is assumed an asset could have earned had it been invested at a realistic rate. For example, money tied up in a checking account has a cost because it could have been invested to earn a return. See also **opportunity cost.**

income. 1) In a business, the amount after netting revenues with expenses. See also **net income** and **operating income.** 2) The salary, wages, or other earnings of individuals.

income averaging. A special method of calculating an individual's federal income tax liability for a year that takes into account the taxable income of past years. Certain restrictions apply to the use of income averaging. This method provides limited tax relief to individuals whose income bunches in a particular year.

income bond. A long-term debt security that pays interest only if income is earned by the issuer. The bonds generally originate in a corporate reorganization.

income from discontinued operations. A category on the income statement that reflects the income, net of taxes, associated with the operating of a segment of the business that was disposed of during the period.

income splitting. The concept of allocating income within a family in order to minimize the total tax liability of the family unit. For example, an individual in the 50 percent tax bracket could lower the family's total tax liability by assigning income to a dependent child in a lower tax bracket. To be legal the primary taxpayer must give the source of the income, e.g. - stocks, bonds, or rental property to the dependent.

income statement. A financial statement showing revenues and expenses and the resulting net income (net loss) for a period of time.

income tax. A tax on net income.

incremental cash flows. The change in cash flows that occur due to altering some financial variable.

incremental cost. The increase in cost from one alternative to another.

incremental revenue. The change in total revenue associated with the addition or subtraction of one unit.

indenture. A formal agreement between the issuer of a bond and the bondholders which specifies the terms of the issue and obligations of the issuer.

independence. The concept in auditing that an auditor is not only in fact free of bias in rendering an opinion, but that (s)he appears to others to have such a relationship with an entity that an objective opinion can be given.

indexed bond. A long-term debt security with payments that are indexed to one or more other values. For example, a bond may be indexed to the price of silver. See also **commodity backed bonds.**

indexing. Adjusting to compensate for the effects of inflation(deflation). For example, certain payments are periodically increased using the consumer price index in order to adjust for increases in the cost of living (inflation).

index numbers. Numerical characterizations of changes that are expressed as relative numbers. Index numbers are displayed as a percentage of some base but the percent sign (%) is never used in their presentation.

indirect costs. Expenditures that occur as a consequence of general overall activities associated with a particular product but which cannot be obviously traced to that product.

indirect labor. Labor associated with manufacturing a product that can not be identified with a particular product and is therefore assigned to manufacturing overhead.

indirect material. Raw material associated with manufacturing a product that cannot be identified with a particular product and is therefore assigned to manufacturing overhead.

Individual Retirement Account. A pension plan established by an individual in which the contributions, subject to limitations, are deductible in determining the individual's taxable income. Proceeds from the plan received after retirement are fully taxable.

inflation. Generally rising prices for goods and services due to a decline in the overall purchasing power of the dollar.

inflation accounting. The concept that the reporting of financial information should take into consideration the decline in purchasing power of the dollar. See also **constant dollar accounting.**

information returns. Tax returns filed by certain classes of taxpayers, e.g. - partnerships, for the purpose of providing information as opposed to the determination of taxes.

inheritance tax. A tax on the right to receive property from a decedent. This type of tax is levied on the heir rather than the estate. Contrast with **estate tax.**

initial direct costs. The incremental costs incurred by a lessor that are directly associated with negotiating and consummating a leasing transaction. For example, legal fees and commissions.

inside director. A member of a board of directors who is otherwise employed by the organization on whose board he or she sits.

insider. A director, officer, or stockholder, owning 10 percent or more of stock outstanding who is able to obtain intimate knowledge of the firm by virtue of his or her official position. An insider is not permitted to take unfair advantage of priviledged information in the trading of securities.

insolvency. The inability of an entity to meet current debt. Currently due liabilities exceed the ability to raise cash to pay the liabilities.

installment sale. Any type of sale in which payment is made in periodic installments over an extended period of time. Under this method gross profit is deferred and recognized in proportion to cash collections in the future.

insure. To transfer to another party the risk of financial loss.

intangible asset. An asset that benefits several

66

future periods and which does not have physical substance. For example, patents, drilling rights.

intercompany elimination. The subtraction of intercompany items in preparing consolidated financial statements. For example, Company A's investment in Company B would be omitted in showing the investments of the combined Company AB.

intercompany profit. The excess of revenue from sales over cost of sales associated with providing goods or services to a related company.

interest. A charge for the use of money.

interest capitalization. See **capitalization of interest.**

interest expense. The cost of borrowing money which is deducted from revenue in determining income.

interest method. The method of determining interest expense/revenue in which the book value of the debt/receivable at the start of the period is multiplied by the effective interest rate for the period. This method results in an increasing or decreasing expense/revenue depending on the change in the book value of the item.

interest rate. The fraction applied to principal for a given period to determine the cost of borrowing money. Usually stated on an annual basis.

interest rate risk. The potential reduction in the market value of an investment due to an increase in interest rates. Long-term investments suffer greater interest rate risk than do investments of short duration.

interim financial statements. Financial statements prepared for a period of time less than the fiscal year. For example, quarterly or monthly statements.

internal audit. An examination conducted by individuals within a firm of the firm's internal control, operational efficiency, or compliance with managements policies. The primary objectives of an internal audit are the prevention and discovery of fraud and the improvement of operational efficiencies.

internal control. The methods and policies within a firm of preventing fraud, safeguarding assets, promoting operational efficiencies, and insuring the dependable recording of data with a minimum of errors.

internal financing. Raising funds within an organization through normal operations. These funds generally consist of retained net income plus noncash expenses.

internal rate of return. The rate of discount that equates the present value of cash inflows with the present value of cash outflows. Normally used to evaluate investment proposals.

Internal Revenue Code. The federal tax law of the United States.

Internal Revenue Service. The agency of the U.S. Treasury Department that administers and enforces the Internal Revenue Code.

interperiod tax allocation. The process of assigning a given year's income tax liability to income statements reflecting several years of operations. The allocation exists when a firm uses one method of accounting for the Internal Revenue Code and another for generally accepted accounting practices. Over a sufficiently long period of time, taxes allocated under each of the methods will be the same.

interpretations. Pronouncements from the Financial Accounting Standards Board (FASB) that explain and amplify previously-issued Statements of Financial Accounting Standards.

interstate. The condition of dying without having a valid will.

intraperiod tax allocation. The allocation of the total tax expense for the year to the event or item which gave raise to it. For example, the tax associated with an extraordinary item is shown with the extraordinary item on the income statement.

inventory. The stock of items held for resale in a merchandising firm, or the raw materials, work in process, or finished goods held by a manufacturing firm.

inventory profit. The profit resulting from carrying inventory at an amount less than its current replacement cost.

inventory reserve. An outdated term for the allowance account used in the lower-of-cost-or-market method of inventory valuation.

inventory turnover. See **ratios.**

inventory valuation. The determination of the amount to be reflected on the balance sheet for inventory. See also, **first-in, first-out** and **last-in, first-out.**

investee company. A corporation whose stock is partially or wholly owned by another company.

investment center. A responsibility center (segment of a business) where the manager is responsible for all applicable revenue, expenses, and investments. Contrast with **cost center** and **profit center.**

investment credit. See **investment tax credit.**

investment tax credit. A specified percentage of the outlay on a qualified asset which may be used to reduce a firm's tax liability. The purpose of the investment tax credit is to stimulate expenditures on capital equipment.

invoice. A form showing the quantity and price of items shipped. A bill.

involuntary bankruptcy. A debtor being forced into bankruptcy court by creditors rather than the debtor voluntarily seeking the protection of the court.

involuntary conversions. The unplanned and untimely disposal of an asset, usually by such means as fire or flood. The accounting treatment is the same as for a normal disposal, that is, a gain if proceeds (from insurance, etc.) exceed book value and a loss if proceeds are less than book value.

IRA. See **Individual Retirement Account.**

IRC. See **Internal Revenue Code.**
IRR. See **internal rate of return.**
IRS. See **Internal Revenue Service.**
ITC. See **investment tax credit.**
itemized deductions. Certain personal subtractions allowed in the determination of taxable income if they exceed the zero bracket amount. Examples include, interest on home mortgages and charitable contributions.

J

job cost sheet. The document used to collect product costs (direct materials, direct labor, and manufacturing overhead) in the job order costing system.

job order costing system. A method of cost accounting in which costs (direct material, direct labor, and manufacturing overhead) are accumulated for a specific task or group of very similar tasks. The task may result in either a product or a service.

joint and several liability. The concept that an obligation may be collected from any one or all of the parties associated with an activity. Especially applicable to the various partners in a general partnership and the husband and wife in a joint tax return.

joint costs. An expenditure that is common to two or more simultaneous activities such as departmental operations or manufacture of products. For example, the cost of the steer is common to both the hamburger and T-bone steak.

joint products. Two or more products that come from the same source or process such that one cannot be produced without the other also being produced. Each of the products has a relatively substantial value. See also **by-products, joint costs,** and **split-off**

point.

joint return. The income tax return filed by a husband and wife in which both are treated as one taxable entity.

joint tenancy with right of survivorship. Joint ownership with each owner having an equal share of the asset and each having the right to sell or give away an ownership interest. Death of a tenant results in his or her share being divided equally among the remaining owners. See also **tenancy by the entirety** and **tenancy in common.**

joint venture. A grouping of two or more individuals or entities to undertake a one-time business objective. Once the undertaking is completed there is no continued relationship among the parties. Joint ventures are treated as partnerships for tax purposes.

journal entry. The means of entering the details of a transaction into the accounting system. Journal entries are made in a journal and later posted to a ledger. The journal entry consists of a date, followed by one or more accounts that are debited and then one or more accounts that are credited. The dollar amount of the debits must equal the dollar amount of the accounts credited. The entry also contains a brief explanation of the transaction.

journalize. To make a journal entry.

journals. Books of original entry in which transactions are recorded in chronological order. The types of journals include:

> **general journal.** The book of original entry for all transactions not meeting the requirements for recording in one of the special journals.

> **special journals.** Journals designed for the recording of specialized classes of transactions. Special journals include:

>> **cash receipts journal.** Journal in which all receipts of cash are recorded.

>> **cash payments (disbursements) journal.** Journal in which all payments of cash

are recorded.

purchases journal. Journal in which all credit purchases are recorded.

sales journal. Journal in which all credit sales are recorded.

judgmental sampling. A sampling technique in which items included in the sample are not selected on a random basis. When this type of sampling is used no statistical statements about percision and confidence can be made.

junior securities. Securities that have a reduced claim on assets and income as compared to one or more other securities the issuer has outstanding.

K

Keogh plan. A retirement plan available for self-employed taxpayers. Such individuals may deduct each year from their gross income up to either 15% of net earnings from self-employment or $15,000, whichever is less.

kiting. The means of taking advantage of the period of time required for a check to clear the banking system in order to cover the "temporary" or permanent shortage of funds. In the process an unrecorded check is written on one bank and cashed at another. Subsequently another unrecorded check is written and deposited to cover the first check, and the process continues in a circular fashion.

L

land. Real estate held for productive use or investment.

lapping. An irregularity that results in the deliberate abstraction of cash receipts. The misappropriation is accomplished by substituting a credit customer's check for cash in a bank deposit and then delaying the recording of the collection in the customers account. Eventually, a payment from a second customer is recorded as a payment from the first customer. This process is continued for subsequent customers.

lapsing schedule. A schedule showing detailed accounting information concerning fixed assets such as the: a) cost of individual items within a class of fixed assets; b) periodic depreciation recognized since purchase; and c) aggregate depreciation recognized since purchase.

last-in, first-out. The method determining the order in which items exit an entity based on the assumption that the most recently acquired items are the first ones consumed or sold. Thus, the items still held by the entity would be the first ones acquired. Contrast with **first-in, first-out.**

LCM. See **lower of cost or market.**

lead time. The time interval between placing an

order and the receipt of the items ordered.

learning curve. The relationship between the level of output (y-axis) and some measure of learning or experience (x-axis) such as time on the job. The basic concept is that it takes less time to complete each successive performance of a task.

lease. A general term for the contract that conveys the right to use by one party (lessee) the property belonging to another (lessor). Depending upon the terms and conditions of the agreement, the lease will have a more specific definition as indicated below:

> **capital lease.** A lease that, in substance, transfers all of the risks and rewards inherent in owning the property to the lessee. The lessee treats the transaction as the acquisition of an asset and incurrence of a liability. The lessor accounts for the lease as a sale or direct financing lease.

> **direct financing lease.** A lease that does not result in a manufacturer's or dealer's profit (difference between present value of the future lease payments and cost to the lessor) and is a capital lease for the lessee. The business advantage to the lessor is that interest is received on the money borrowed.

> **leverage lease.** A lease in which a major portion of the acquisition cost of the property is provided by a third party (as opposed to the lessor).

> **operating lease.** A lease in which the risks and rewards of ownership remain with the lessor. The payments are recorded by the lessee as rental expense and by the lessor as rental income.

> **sale and leaseback lease.** The sale of property by an owner to a purchaser who then leases it to the original owner.

> **sales type lease.** A lease that results in a

manufacturer's or dealer's profit or loss (difference between present value of the future lease payments and cost to the lessor) and is a capital lease for the lessee.

leaseback. See **sale and leaseback.**

leasehold. Property used by the lessee in a lease agreement.

leasehold improvement. Enhancements made to leased property by the lessee that usually revert to the lessor at the end of the lease. The cost of such improvements is shown either in the plant, property, and equipment section of the balance sheet or as intangible assets. The cost should be depreciated over the remaining life of the lease or the useful life of the improvements, whichever is shorter.

lease term. The period of time a lease is to be in effect without the right of cancellation.

least squares method. A statistical technique of fitting a line to a set of points so as to minimize the sum of the squared deviations between the points and the line. This technique develops the equation that defines the relationship between the two variables.

ledger. The book of all of the accounts of a business. The accounts are shown in the order they appear on the balance sheet; assets, liabilities, and owners' equity followed by revenue and expense accounts.

legal capital. The minimum investment by owners that must be left in a corporation for the protection of creditors. In most states legal capital is defined as par value or its equivalent.

legal liability. 1) The responsibility for an obligation that can be enforced by law. 2) The contractual obligation of a CPA to his client and certain third parties dictating that he perform an audit with the due care required of an individual in his profession.

lessee. The individual or organization which, through a lease agreement, acquires exclusive

77

right to the use of an asset.

lessor. The owner of a leased asset who receives payments from the asset's user.

letter of credit. A statement by a bank that it will honor a draft written by a specific party provided that certain conditions are satisfied.

letter of representation. See **representation letter**.

leverage. The magnifying effect of changes in sales upon changes in income that is caused by the utilization of assets and financing with fixed charges.

levy. 1) The amount of taxes, special assessments, or service charges imposed by a governmental unit. 2) The act of imposing taxes, special assessments, or service charges to support governmental activities.

liability. An obligation to either pay an amount of money or to provide some service or good.

lien. The right to control property owned by another party until a legal debt owed by the property owner is paid to the lienholder.

LIFO. See **last-in, first-out**.

like-kind exchanges. See **non-monetary exchanges**.

limited audit. A service once offered by CPA's but no longer available. See **review** and **compilation**.

limited liability. Legal protection to the owners of a firm that limits their financial losses to no more than the amount they invested.

limited partner. A partner in a business enterprise who is responsible for debts only to the extent of his or her investment. Limited partners are generally not active in management of the business.

limited partnership. A partnership composed of one general partner and one or more limited partners.

linear programming. A mathematical means of obtaining an optimal solution. For example, maximizing revenue or minimizing costs subject to a complex set of quantifiable constraints.

line budgeting. Preparing budgets using the same account classifications for revenue and expense items as utilized in accounting reports.

line item budget. See **line budgeting.**

line of credit. An agreement whereby a firm may borrow up to a prearranged maximum amount of money from a financial institution for a given period of time.

liquid asset. An item of value that can be turned into cash in a short period of time with no more than a small concession in price.

liquidating dividend. See **dividend.**

liquidation. The process of closing a business by sale of assets, settlement of debts, and distribution of residual assets to the owners.

liquidation value. The amount of cash that could be expected on the sale of the assets of a firm during a distress sale.

liquidity. The ability to meet current financial obligations as they come due.

liquidity ratios. Financial ratios that measure the ability of a firm to meet its short-term obligations. Current ratio, inventory turnover, and receivables turnover are examples of liquidity ratios. Also see **ratios.**

listed securities. Securities that are traded on one or more of the organized securities exchanges such as the New York Stock Exchange, American Stock Exchange, or Pacific Stock Exchange.

lock-box system. A procedure for speeding the collection of receivables by having customers send remittances to a post office box. The firm's bank is authorized to pick up the payments (often several times per day) and deposit them in the company's account.

long-lived assets. Assets that are expected to last over several years, especially plant, property, and equipment.

long-term capital gain/loss. The gain (loss) resulting from the sale of a capital asset. For individuals, 60 percent of such gains may be excluded from income for tax purposes.

Losses may be offset against gains. Non-corporate taxpayers may, to a limited extent established by formula, recognize losses as a short-term loss and offset against ordinary income.

long-term debt. See **long-term liabilities.**

long-term liabilities. Debt obligations that are not due to be settled within one year. See also **bonds.**

loss. 1) The excess of book value over selling price. 2) An outflow of an asset that does not produce revenue. 3) The excess of expenses over revenue on an income statement.

loss carryback/carryforward. The offset of a current year's loss against profits of the three prior years (carrybacks) and, if necessary, against a specified number (currently 15) of future years (carryforwards).

lower of cost or market. A method of asset valuation that allows a departure from the cost principle in that market value may be used if it is less than cost. Used frequently with inventory and marketable securities.

LP. See **linear programming.**

LTCG. See **long-term capital gain/loss.**

LTCL. See **long-term capital gain/loss.**

lump-sum purchase. The acquisition of several identifiable assets for one amount with no price being associated with any individual items in the group.

M

machine hour. A method of allocating costs on the basis of machine hours utilized.

maintenance. Expenditures required to enable an asset to achieve its original expected useful life.

maintenance lease. A lease agreement in which the lessor (owner) pays for all maintenance of the leased asset.

maker. An individual who signs and promises to pay on a negotiable instrument.

management accounting. An area of accounting dealing with records and reports that are meant for use by internal management. Examples include performance reports, budgets, and special reports relating to specific operating areas.

management advisory services. A consulting service offered by CPA firms to assist a company's management in increasing its productivity.

management by exception. The concept of focusing attention on phases of operations in which major deviations from expected results are occurring. Areas that are running smoothly are ignored.

management information system. The organization plan and procedures that provide internal and external information in a timely manner to assist a firm's decision makers.

managerial accounting. The field of accounting concerned with the gathering and providing of accounting information used within an organization for decision making, planning, and control. Contrast with **financial accounting.**

manufacturing cost. See **product cost.**

manufacturing overhead. Product costs other than direct materials and direct labor. Manufacturing overhead usually has both a variable and fixed portion and typically includes indirect material (factory supplies), indirect labor, maintenance, depreciation on factory buildings and equipment, utilities, and the like.

marginal analysis. A technique of analyzing variables, such as cost and revenue, by utilizing differences or changes rather than absolute amounts. An example of marginal analysis would be to determine the extra cost and extra revenue involved in producing and selling another unit of output to determine if it was profitable to do so.

marginal cost. The increase in total cost associated with the next unit of activity.

marginal revenue. The increase in total revenue as a result of selling one additional unit.

marginal tax rate. The tax that must be paid on an additional dollar of income. This is often referred to as a taxpayer's tax bracket.

markdown. A reduction in the original selling price.

marketable securities. A classification of current assets composed of securities that meet both of the following criteria; may be sold quickly because a ready market exists and managements only reason for investing is to put idle cash to more productive use. Treasury bills, commercial paper, and negotiable certificates of deposit are examples of marketable securities.

market value. The price at which an item would trade in a fair market.

markup. The amount added to the cost of an item to determine its selling price. Markup is usually expressed as a percentage of cost.

MAS. See **management advisory services.**

master file. A file containing the permanent records of a firm and its activities.

matching. The concept of income determination that compares the cost of benefits received (expenses) with benefits received (revenues). This concept results in recognizing related expenses and revenues in the same accounting period.

material inventory. See **direct material inventory.**

materiality. The concept concerned with when items should be included or excluded from financial statements. When an item is large enough to influence a decision then it is appropriate that the item be disclosed.

maturity date. The date on which a loan must be repaid.

maturity value. The amount required to satisfy an obligation when it becomes due.

merchandise inventory. Goods acquired and held for resale. contrast with **finished goods inventory.**

merger. A combination of two or more firms into a single surviving entity. The acquiring corporation acquires the assets and liabilities of the merged firms.

minimum tax. The concept that all federal taxpayers, particularly those with large incomes, should pay a fair share of the total tax burden. The procedure for determining the additional tax liability, while complex, is essentially one of levying a special tax on categories of items that receive preferential treatment for tax purposes. See also **tax preference items.**

minority interest. In a consolidation, that portion of a subsidiary not owned by the controlling company or other members of the consolidation group.

MIS. See **management information system.**

miscellaneous expense. A category on the income statement indicating incidental expenditures not easily placed into one of the major classifications of expenses such as selling or administrative.

mixed costs. Costs that have both a fixed and a variable component. Sometimes called semi-variable costs.

modified accrual basis. The departure from the strict interpretation of the concept of accrual accounting in the determination of income. Primarily utilized in governmental accounting by recognizing revenues only when they become available.

monetary assets. Assets such as cash, accounts receivable, and other items having a contractual claim to a fixed amount of cash. During periods of inflation the holding of monetary assets will result in a loss of purchasing power.

monetary liabilities. Current obligations such as accounts payable and notes payable as well as long-term obligations such as bonds payable and preferred stock that are payable in fixed sums. During periods of inflation the holding of monetary liabilities will result in a gain in purchasing power.

money market. Financial markets in which short-term securities such as Treasury bills, certificates of deposit, and commercial paper are traded.

mortgage. A lien against specified real property as security for a loan.

mortgage bond. A long-term debt security which gives its holder first claim on real property that is being used as collateral.

moving average. A method of accounting for the costs of items purchased at different prices. The average unit cost is recomputed after each additional acquisition and costs of items sold are at the average. Most frequently used for inventory but could be used for other items.

moving expense. In tax accounting, the unreimbursed costs involved when an individual moves from one job location to another. Subject to certain limitations and restrictions, moving expenses are subtracted from gross income in calculating adjusted gross income.

multinational corporation. A corporation with diverse operations in many different countries.

multiple regression. A statistical technique that measures the amount of change in a dependent variable associated with changes in two or more independent variables. Utilized as a means of developing models concerned with the behavior of costs.

municipal bond. A debt security issued by a state, city, or political subdivision. Interest received by municipal bondholders is exempt from federal income tax and often from state and local income taxes as well.

N

NAA. See **National Association of Accountants.**
National Association of Accountants. An
 organization of individuals interested in
 management and cost accounting. The NAA
 supports the Certificate in Management
 Accounting (CMA) program and publishes
 <u>Management Accounting.</u>
negative goodwill. When purchasing a firm,
 the excess of the value of identifiable assets
 acquired over the purchase price.
negligence. The failure to exercise due care.
 Used in describing the performance of auditors.
 See also **ordinary negligence** and **gross
 negligence.**
negotiable instrument. A financial instrument
 that may be transferred at any price agreeable
 to the parties involved in the transaction.
 Examples include checks, drafts, and certain
 certificates of deposit.
negotiated offering. The process of negotiating
 the terms of a new security issue with an
 investment banker (underwriter).
net assets. Total assets minus total liabilities.
net income. The excess of revenues over all
 expenses for a given period of time. This is
 the final income figure that appears on the
 income statement.
net operating loss. An excess of allowable

deductions over gross income. A net operating loss may be carried back three years and carried forward seven years in order to offset past or future taxable income.

net present value. The present value of cash inflows minus the present value of cash outflows when both are discounted at the required rate. This is a tool for evaluating an investment proposal.

net proceeds. The amount of cash or other assets or services received from the disposal of property or sale of securities less the costs associated with the act of disposing of the property or selling the securities. The adjusted historical cost is not utilized in the calculation.

net profit. See **net income.**

net purchases. The cost of inventory items purchased less cash discounts, returns and allowances, plus freight-in.

net realizable value. 1) The estimated selling price of an item of inventory minus the expected costs to complete and dispose of the item. 2) The amount of receivables that are expected to be collected after considering uncollectible accounts.

net sales. Gross sales less cash discounts, freight-out, and returns and allowances.

net working capital. See **working capital.**

net worth. See **owners' equity.**

NI. See **net income.**

NOL. See **net operating loss.**

nominal account. An account used during an accounting period to collect amounts relating to that period. Also called temporary accounts, they begin the period with a zero balance and are closed into owners' equity at the end of the period. Nominal accounts include revenue and expense, dividend, and closing accounts such as income summary.

nominal interest rate. The stated rate of interest in a credit contract. This may be different than the effective rate or the real rate.

nonassessable capital stock. Capital stock that is fully paid and not subject to any additional assessments.

noncash charge. An expense that is deducted for tax purposes, but which requires no cash outlay. Depreciation is an example of a noncash charge.

noncontributory pension plan. A pension plan in which all of the cost is borne by the employer.

nonmonetary exchange. The process of acquiring an asset by trading a currently-owned asset. Sometimes another asset, called boot (usually cash), is also paid or received in addition to the major assets involved.

nonmonetary items. Financial statement items that are stated in dollar amounts that can change with changes in the purchasing power of the dollar. Examples include inventories, operating assets, and common stock outstanding. Contrast with **monetary assets** and **monetary liabilities.**

nonprice competition. Competition based upon either real or perceived quality differences rather than price. This normally involves significant marketing expenditures on the part of the organization providing the good or service.

nonprofit accounting. The accounting procedures and techniques used in organizations such as governments, churches, and charitable institutions that traditionally do not seek profit as a major goal.

nonrecourse note. A note in which the creditor does not have the legal right to force the borrower to pay if the terms of the note are not honored.

nonrefundable debt. An issue of debt that may not be called by the issuer prior to maturity in order to replace it with a new issue.

nonroutine decisions. Decisions that are not of a recurring nature.

no-par stock. Common stock that does not have a

par or stated value. See also **par value** and **stated value.**

normal cost. The cost associated with a pension plan subsequent to the date of adoption or the date of an amendment to the plan

note. A written agreement between two parties where one promises to pay another a specific sum of money on a certain date, usually plus a specified amount of interest.

note payable. A written promise to pay a specified amount on a specific date, usually plus a specified amount of interest.

note receivable. A written promise from another party to pay a specified amount on a specific date, usually plus a specified amount of interest.

notes receivable-discounted. Notes owned by an entity and sold prior to maturity such that the net amount received is less than what would have been received had the notes been held to maturity.

NPV. See **net present value.**

NR. See **note receivable.**

NSF. Non sufficient funds.

N S F check. A customer's check that has been accepted as payment and deposited but did not clear on presentation because the customer's bank balance was less than the amount of the check.

O

objectivity. The concept that financial statements are based on factual and verifiable transactions rather than subjective judgment. Thus, two accountants with similar education and experience would record a given transaction in essentially the same manner.

obligation. Any requirement either to pay an amount of money or provide some service or good due to a liability or indebtness.

obsolescence. A permanent decline in an asset's value due to such factors as diminished customer demand or changing technology.

off-balance-sheet financing. Raising funds in such a manner that no additional liabilities are clearly displayed on the balance sheet.

offering price. The price at which a security is sold to the public.

officer. A principal executive of an organization. Officers normally include a president, vice-president(s), secretary, and treasurer. Officers may or may not be members of the firm's board of directors.

open account. A trade credit arrangement in which goods are shipped in the absence of a formal debt agreement between the seller and buyer.

opening balance. See **beginning balance**.

operating assets. The assets of an organization that contribute to the normal flow of income from regular operations. Usually limited to plant, property and equipment.

operating budget. The financial plan for revenues and expenses incurred in the regular activities of the firm. Essentially a projected income statement.

operating costs. Expenditures such as wages, utilities, and raw materials that are necessary to conduct the regular activities of the firm.

operating expenses. See **operating costs.**

operating income. The excess of revenues over operating expenses. It does not include income such as interest and dividends or expenses such as interest, that are not associated with normal operations.

operating lease. A short-term lease that is frequently cancellable and does not fully amortize the asset. The lessor is normally responsible for maintenance, tax payments, and insurance.

operating leverage. A measure of the extent to which a firm's operations involve fixed costs. A firm with high operating leverage will experience a large change in operating income given a relatively small change in sales.

operating loss. The condition that exists when operating expenses exceed operating revenues. Contrast with **operating income.**

operational audit. See **auditing.**

operations research. The use of mathematical and statistical methods to analyze data to be used in decision making.

opinion. 1) The written statement of a CPA concerning the audit of the financial statements of an entity. 2) A statement by the now defunct Accounting Principles Board concerning the procedures, practices, or techniques to be followed in reporting a particular type of transaction.

opportunity cost. The alternative earnings associated with giving up the next best course of action to the one actually chosen.

ordinary annuity. The periodic payment or receipt

of a constant amount of money at a constant interest rate in which the payments or receipts occur at the end of the period. Also see **annuity due.**

ordinary income. 1) Profit from the regular, normal, and recurring activities of a firm. 2) For tax purposes, that income not eligible for capital gains treatment.

ordinary negligence. The unwillful failure to exercise due care because of lack of experience, training, or oversight. Contrast with **fraud** and **gross negligence.**

organizational cost. The expenditures, such as legal fees, incorporation fees, and stock issue costs, associated with establishing a business. These costs are capitalized as an intangible asset and amortized over future periods.

original cost. See **historical cost.**

original issue discount. The excess of the face value of a bond over the selling price at the time of issue. The discount is amortized as an expense over the life of the bond.

other assets. A classification on the balance sheet indicating the adjusted historical cost of miscellaneous resources owned that cannot be clearly assigned to another category of assets.

out-of-pocket costs. Expenditures associated with carrying out a particular activity.

outside director. A member of an organization's board of directors who is not also a past or present employee of the organization.

outstanding stock. Stock that has been issued and is currently owned by entities external to the firm issuing the stock.

overapplied overhead. The excess of manufacturing overhead assigned to work-in-process inventory over the actual amount of overhead incurred during the period.

overdraft. A check written for more than the balance in the bank account.

overhead cost. See **manufacturing overhead.**

overhead rate. The ratio of the expected total manufacturing overhead for a period to the amount of some factor believed to be directly related to the incurrence. Direct labor dollars, direct labor hours, and machine hours are frequently considered to have a direct bearing on the incurrence of overhead. The overhead rate is used to assign overhead to the work-in-process inventory.

overhead volume variance. See **variance.**

owners' equity. That portion of a firm's asset costs contributed by the owners as opposed to creditors. Consists of the amounts actually invested by the owners plus profits retained in the business.

owners of record. See **holders of record.**

P

PA. See public accountant.

paid-in capital. See contributed capital.

paid-in capital - excess over par value. See contributed capital - in excess of par or stated value.

paid-in surplus. See contributed capital - in excess of par or stated value.

paper profit. See unrealized gain.

parent company. A company that owns a controlling interest (more than 50%) of the voting stock of another company.

participating preferred stock. An unusual type of preferred stock that, in addition to its regular dividend, may receive additional dividends from residual earnings according to some specified formula.

partnership. An association of two or more persons who combine capital and/or services to own and operate a business, usually for profit. Differs from a corporation in that ownership cannot be transferred and maintain the entity. Also, each partner may be held liable for an amount greater than his(her) investment. See also limited partnership.

par value. 1) A nominal value appearing on a stock certificate which represents the minimum amount to be paid to the issuing corporation by the original investor. 2) The maturity value of a bond, usually $1,000.

passed dividend. An expected dividend that was not declared. The term is normally used to describe preferred stock dividends.

past costs. See **sunk costs.**

past service cost. The cost resulting from consideration given to years of service of employees prior to the adopting of a pension plan.

patent. The exclusive right granted by the U.S. Patent Office to produce, use, or otherwise control a product or process for 17 years. Shown on the balance sheet as an intangible asset.

payable. An unpaid liability.

payback method. An evaluation of long-term investments in which the time period required to recover the initial investment is the major consideration. Calculated by dividing the initial outlay by the annual cash flow.

payback period. The length of time required to recover an investment's initial outlay.

payee. The individual who will be paid from either a check or note.

payment in kind. Payment made in goods or services rather than cash.

payout ratio. See **dividend payout ratio.**

payroll. A record showing the details of employee compensation for a period of time. Includes deductions from employees' pay as well as employer paid items such as health insurance and F.I.C.A. contributions.

payroll register. See **payroll.**

payroll taxes. The taxes associated with the earning of income through salary or wages and withheld by the employer. For example, Social Security taxes.

pension expense. The cost of a pension plan for a given accounting period.

pension fund. Resources accumulated by a firm or its agent for the purpose of paying benefits established by the firm's pension plan.

pension liability. 1) An actuarial concept

representing the economic obligation for future cash payments to retirees under a pension plan. 2) The excess of amounts expensed over amounts contributed to a pension fund.

pension plan. A firm's formal policy of providing resources to employees upon retirement. May also include disability and death benefits.

PE ratio. See **price-earnings ratio.**

percentage-of-completion method. A method of accounting for long-term projects in which the portion of the total revenues and costs associated with a specific time period are recognized in that period. Recognition is based on the portion (percentage) of the work completed, that is, the ratio of costs for this period to total estimated costs for the project.

percent depletion. See **depletion.**

period costs. Expenditures that are more closely identified with measured time intervals than the delivery of goods or the providing of services. Selling and administrative costs are examples of period costs and, as such, appear on the income statement as expenses in the periods in which they are incurred.

periodic inventory system. A means of determining the amount of goods in inventory at the end of an accounting period by physically counting and pricing items.

periodicity. The concept that items of revenue and expense should be allocated to specific periods in order to prepare financial statements at regular intervals.

perk. See **perquisite.**

permanent difference. The situation that arises when items of revenue or expense are recognized for tax purposes but not accounting purpose or for accounting purposes and not tax purposes. For example, interest income on municipal bonds is recognized as interest income for accounting purposes but is never recognized for tax purposes. Contrast with **timing differences.**

perpetual inventory system. A method of recording

inventory that provides for a continuous record of items acquired and sold. At any given point in time the balance in the inventory will be shown as the beginning balance plus acquisitions minus sales.

perpetuity. A series of equal payments (annuity) that continue indefinitely.

perquisite. An additional benefit provided to someone due to his or her position. Examples include a country club membership, a private secretary, and a corner office with a window. Also called a perk.

personal exemption. An amount, currently $1,000.00 for federal income tax returns, that is exempt from income tax. An exemption is allowed for each taxpayer, spouse (if filing a joint return), and dependent. Additional exemptions are permitted for taxpayers over 65, or blind, or both.

personal property. All resources other than real property (land, land improvements, and buildings).

PERT. See **program evaluation and review technique.**

petty cash. A special cash fund used for the payment of immaterial items when payment by check is not feasible.

PHC. Personal holding company.

physical inventory. A procedure for determining the amount of inventory on hand by counting the items and multiplying by unit cost.

plant and equipment to long-term debt. See **ratios.**

plant and equipment turnover. See **ratios.**

plant, property, and equipment. The long-lived assets of a firm that are used in the production of revenue and not held for resale. Specifically, plant equals building, property equals land, and equipment equals machinery. See also **operating assets.**

pledged asset. An asset that is being used to secure a loan.

pledging of accounts receivable. See **assignment**

of accounts receivable.

P & L statement. See **income statement.**

pooling of interests method. A method of combining, in an accounting sense, two or more previously existing companies into one ownership interest. The combination takes the form of changes in ownership rights (stock), as opposed to a cash transaction. The book values of the assets and equities of the combined entity are the same as the total book values of the combining entities and no revaluation takes place. Contrast with **purchase method.**

portfolio. A combination of financial and/or real assets.

postdate. To date a document at the time the document is written but with a datae that is in the future.

posting. The process of transferring the amounts shown in the journals to an appropriate ledger account.

PP & E. See **plant, property, and equipment.**

predetermined overhead rate. See **overhead rate.**

preemptive right. The provision of some firms which entitles common stockholders to maintain their share of ownership by having the opportunity to purchase a proportionate amount of new common stock or securities convertible into common stock.

preferred stock. An equity security with a claim on earnings and assets that is senior to that of common stockholders but follows the claims of creditors. Although most preferred issues pay fixed dividends and carry no voting rights, there are exceptions. Also see **participating preferred stock.**

premium on bonds. The excess of sale price over face or par value due to the coupon or contract rate of interest being higher than the market rate of interest at time of sale.

premium on common or preferred stock. See **contributed capital-in excess of par or stated value.**

prepaid expenses. Expenditures for services, such

as rent and insurance, that will be received and consumed after the date of payment. Shown as a current asset on the balance sheet.

present value. The current worth of a sum or stream of money to be received on some future date(s) when the future payment(s) are discounted at a specified rate.

price-earnings ratio. A common stock measure of the number of dollars investors are willing to pay for a dollar of earnings. Calculated by dividing the current market price of a firm's common stock by current or expected earnings per share.

price level adjustments. Changes made to original data, usually shown at cost, to present the effects of changes in the purchasing power of the dollar.

primary earnings per share. Earnings per share adjusted for the impact of common stock equivalents. This is the first earnings per share calculation shown for a company with a complex capital structure.

prime cost. Direct materials plus direct materials. Prime cost excludes all overhead.

prime rate. The interest rate that banks charge their most credit-worthy customers on short-term loans. This is a benchmark rate that influences rates on many short-term loans.

principal. 1) The amount of money on which interest accrues. 2) An individual who has authorized someone else to represent him in business dealings.

prior period adjustment. Income and expense items related to previous periods that are treated as adjustments to the beginning balance in retained earnings and do not appear on the income statement. Errors constitute the major type of transaction receiving this treatment.

prior service cost. The cost associated with a pension plan as a result of giving consideration to years of employees' service prior to the amendment of the plan.

private pension plan. An arrangement between a

company and its employees in which the company provides periodic benefits that are based on company policies and determined in advance.

proceeds. The amount of cash other assets or services received from the disposal of property or the sale of securities.

process costing. A method of cost accounting used when production results in a continuous stream of similar items that pass through a series of consecutive processes or steps (for example, a paper mill). Costs are accumulated through these steps for a given period and then are assigned to a completed unit based on total costs divided by equivalent units of work produced. Contrast with **job order costing.**

product costs. Expenditures that are more closely associated with products than periods of time. These expenditures are not treated as expenses in the period in which they are incurred but rather are inventoried as assets until the products are sold. Only then are the costs expensed so that they appear on the income statement. Product costs are identified so closely with a product that, if the product was not manufactured, the costs generally would not be incurred. Contrast with **period costs.**

production volume variance. See **variance.**

product line reporting. See **segment reporting.**

product mix. The combination of products sold in a multiple product firm.

profit. The excess of revenues over costs.

profitability index. A measure of relative profitability that is calculated by dividing an investment project's initial cost into the present value of its expected cash flows.

profit and loss statement. Income statement.

profit center. A segment of a business in which the manager is responsible for both revenues and costs.

profit margin. A financial ratio that measures the portion of each sales dollar carried to a firm's bottom line. It is calculated by dividing total sales into net income after taxes.

pro forma statements. Financial statements prepared on the basis of certain assumptions for example, statements showing budgeted figures or the effects of two companies merging.

program evaluation and review technique. A planning method that identifies a network of sequential events with the estimated time of each.

programmed costs. Costs that will be incurred for a period of time due to management actions and essentially fixed during the period.

program planning budgeting system. A comprehensive planning and budgeting procedure concerned with the specific activities (programs) established to achieve the goals of the organization. Used especially in the public sector.

progressive tax. A tax in which the rate of taxation increases as the variable to be taxed (normally income or asset value) increases. The federal income tax is an example of a progressive tax.

promissory note. A written promise to pay a specific amount of money at some future date or on demand. The note may be made out to a specific party or to bearer.

property dividend. See **dividend.**

proprietorship. A business enterprise with a single owner who has sole right to the profits and is personally responsible for the liabilities.

prospectus. A condensed form of a firm's registration statement that is made available to potential buyers of a new security issue. The document describes the securities and the organization issuing the securities to the extent that investors can make their own evaluation.

protective covenant. See **covenant.**

protest fee. A charge by a financial institution for a note that is not paid at maturity.

proxy. A power of attorney signed by a stockholder that assigns to another person or persons the right to vote the stockholder's shares.

proxy fight. An attempt by an outside group to obtain control of a firm's management by acquiring proxies from stockholders.

prudent investment. An investment that would be acquired using the norms of a prudent man. Generally applied to keep individuals acting as fiduciaries from engaging in speculative activities.

public accountant. An accountant who offers his or her professional services to the public. The term normally is not used to include certified public accountants.

public accounting. The offering to the public by any accountant of his or her other independent accounting services. Used especially for those who are not CPAs.

purchase commitment losses. Losses due to a decline in the market value of inventory items that, on a prior date, a firm contracted to acquire at a fixed price.

purchase method. A method of combining, in an accounting sense, two or more previously existing companies. The combination takes the form of one entity purchasing (for cash as opposed to exchange of stock) the other. The assets and equities of the acquired company are revalued to fair market on the date of acquisition and carried at this new value on the books of the acquiring company. The acquiring company also reports the results of operations of the acquired company as its own. Contrast with **pooling of interests method.**

purchase order. A form showing that a firm's management has authorized the acquisition of specific assets.

purchase returns and allowances. An account showing reductions in the cost of inventory because of items returned to the vendor or because of reductions in original cost due to defects.

purchases. 1) Items acquired as additions to asset accounts. 2) Under the periodic inventory system, an account debited when items are acquired for resale.

purchases discounts. An account showing reductions from invoice price due to making payments within a stated cash discount period.

purchases journal. See **journals.**

purchasing power gains. The favorable effect of holding net monetary liabilities during a period of inflation or net monetary assets during a period of deflation.

purchasing power loss. The unfavorable effect of holding net monetary assets during a period of inflation or net monetary liabilities during a period of deflation.

PV. See **present value.**

Q

qualified opinion. An audit opinion by a certified public accountant which states that some specified aspect of the audit prevents an unqualified opinion.

quality control. A process of inspection or examination or an operation to determine and prevent deviations from an established specification.

quantity discount. A reduction in price because of the volume purchased or sold.

quantity variance. See **material quantity variance** under **variance**.

quarterly report. An abbreviated form of annual financial statements issued, usually on an unaudited basis, every three months.

quasi-reorganization. A procedure that permits a corporation with a negative balance in retained earnings (but otherwise financially sound) to get a "fresh start" in an accounting sense. The procedure must be approved by stockholders and establishes a zero balance in retained earnings by writing down overvalued assets and writing down paid-in capital accounts.

quick assets. Very liquid assets such as cash, market securities, and current receivables.

quick ratio. See **ratios**.

R

random sample. See sampling.

rate of exchange. 1) The rate at which shares of an acquiring firm are traded for shares of an acquired firm during a merger or acquisition. 2) The rate at which a unit of one currency can be exchanged for a unit of another currency.

rate of return. The annual percentage return after taxes an investment provides or is expected to provide. Also see ratios.

ratio analysis. The computation and evaluation of financial and operating data expressed in ratio form. Comparisons may be made over time or with the same ratios for other firms or industries.

ratios. Ratios are catagorized according to the major types of information they tend to convey. The following are frequently-used ratios classified as to their primary areas of emphasis.

short-run solvency measurements.
accounts receivable turnover = credit sales divided by average accounts receivable balance. The number of times receivables were fully collected and replenished during the period. This is a measure of a firm's credit terms and the quality of its receivables.

acid test = (current assets - inventories) divided by current liabilities. This indicates the ability to meet short-term obligations without having to rely on inventory, a current asset that often has limited liquidity. Also called the quick ratio.

average collection period = days in a year divided by accounts receivable turnover. This measures the average number of days that elapse from date of sale to date of collection.

current ratio = current assets divided by current liabilities. Indicates the ability of a firm to meet its current obligations.

days sales in inventory = days in a year divided by inventory turnover. Indicates the number of days required to sell the inventory one time.

days sales outstanding = ending accounts receivable balance divided by average daily sales for the preceeding period. This indicates the age of a firm's receivables.

inventory turnover = cost of goods sold divided by average inventory. Measures the number of times inventory was replenished during the period.

quick ratio. See **acid test.**

long-run solvency measurements

creditors' equity ratio = total liabilities divided by total assets. This measures the percent of assets financed by creditors and is often known as the debt ratio.

debt to equity ratio = total liabilities divided by stockholders' equity. Indicates funds supplied by creditors in relation to funds provided by owners.

fixed charge coverage = earnings before taxes and deductible fixed charges divided by deductible + (nondeductible fixed charges)(1 divided by 1-t) where t = effective tax rate. This indicates the ability of a firm to meet all of its fixed expenses. Sometimes, such as in SEC filings, preferred dividends are included in fixed charges.

plant and equipment to long-term debt = net plant and equipment divided by long-term debt. This indicates the adequacy of asset protection to long-term creditors.

plant and equipment turnover = net sales divided by average net plant and equipment. Measures the dollar amount of sales produced by a dollar of investment in plant and equipment. Sometimes referred to as fixed asset turnover.

stockholdelrs' equity ratio = stockholders' equity divided by total assets. This measures the portion of assets financed by owners.

times interest earned = income before interest and taxes divided by annual interest expense. Indicates the ability of the firm to meet its interest obligations.

earnings power and growth potential measurements

earnings yield rate = earnings per share divided by market price per share. Indicates the return to stockholders from corporate earnings (paid in dividends and retained in the firm) on the basis of the current value of their shares.

return on common stockholder's equity = net income available to common stockholders divided by owners' equity - par value of preferred stock. Indicates the earning power of owners' investment.

return on total assets = net income divided by average total assets. Indicates earning power of assets and is frequently termed return on investment.

raw materials. Ingredients or component parts of a product that are vital to production.

raw materials inventory. The supply of raw materials on hand at any particular point in time.

R & D. See **research and development costs.**

RE. See retained earnings.

real accounts. Permanent accounts that continue from one period to another. For example, balance sheet accounts.

realization. 1) A general term referring to the fact that an economic event or transaction has been consumated. 2) The process of converting noncash items into cash or receivables. See also **realized gain or loss** and **unrealized gain or loss.**

realized gain. The result of a completed transaction in which the proceeds exceed the book value of the item involved. For example, an asset with a book value of $4,000 when sold for $5,500 results in a realized gain of $1,500. Contrast with **unrealized gain.**

realized loss. The result of a completed transaction in which the book value of the item exceeds the proceeds. For example, when bonds payable with a book value of $1,500,000 are repurchased for $1,700,000 the transaction results in a realized loss of $200,000.

real property. Land, improvements, and buildings.

rebate. An allowance or refund on a portion of the price paid.

recapture. The giving up or cancellation of a tax benefit received from a deduction or a credit taken in a prior period.

recapture of depreciation. On the disposal of depreciable property, the recognition and classification of some of the gain as ordinary income as opposed to all of the gain receiving long-term capital gains treatment. Recapture of depreciation exists to prevent a taxpayer from converting depreciation deductions into an eventual long-term capital gain.

recapture of investment tax credit. The recognition of some of the previously claimed investment tax credits as an additional tax liability. This occurs when an asset is held for a shorter period than was originally estimated when the tax credit was claimed.

receipt. Written acknowledgement that something has been received.

receipts. Funds received from the sale of goods and services.

receivable. A claim of one entity against another for money, goods, or services.

recognition. The formal recording of an item or event into the financial records of an entity. For example, a decline in the market value of inventory may be recognized by writing down the asset. Contrast with **realization.** A transaction may be recognized even though there has been no realization.

reconciliation. The study, evaluation, and determination of the difference between two amounts or balances. For example the reconciliation of the difference between cash balance as shown by the firm's books and as shown by its bank statement.

record. 1) The act of entering information into a system, such as making a journal entry. 2) A document that contains stored information.

record date. See **date of record.**

red herring. A preliminary prospectus provided to potential investors of a new security issue. The name derives from a statement on the cover that is printed in red ink and warns that the registration statement has not yet been approved by the Securities and Exchange Commission.

reference file. A file that is relatively permanent and contains data, usually in tabular form, such as inventory items and prices, that are used in processing.

refunding. Retiring an existing issue of securities with the funds raised from the sale of a new issue. Often utilized to retire bond issues after interest rates have dropped.

registered security. A security whose owner is registered on the books of the issuing organization. A registered security must be endorsed by the registered owner in order to be transferred.

registrar. A financial institution selected to record the sale and ownership of an organization's security issue.

registration. The process of informing the Securities and Exchange Commission, through a written document, of the material facts relating to a new issue of securities.

registration statement. A written document filed with the Securities and Exchange Commission prior to selling a new issue of securities. The lengthy document contains material facts relating to the issue, the issuer, and the underwriting agreement.

regression analysis. A statistical method of examining the relationship between a dependent variable and one or more independent variables.

regulations. A term which is often used to refer to Treasury Department regulations (Regs) or pronouncements by the Internal Revenue Service setting forth how the Internal Revenue Code is to be interpreted.

reinvestment rate. The rate of return which cash flows from an investment are able to earn upon reinvestment.

relative sales value method. A method of assigning joint or common costs in proportion to an item's ability to generate revenue.

relevant cost. A concept of cost used in choosing among alternatives. Only those costs that will occur in the future and will differ among alternatives are used for to decision making.

relevant range. The span of activity over which certain estimates, especially fixed costs, remain constant or true.

removal costs. The costs associated with disposal of an item.

reorder point. The quantity level at which additional consumable items must be ordered. This level should consider the time required for the supplier to fill and ship the order as well as a reserve to prevent running out of the item.

reorganization. A significant change in the financial structure of a corporation through merger or consolidation with another corporation or group of associated corporations.

replacement cost. The current cost required to replace the service potential of an existing asset. The emphasis is not on replacing the asset with a new one but rather with an asset with identical future service capabilities.

replacement method of depreciation. A method of depreciation in which depreciation expense is only recognized when an original asset is replaced. The amount of the depreciation expense recognized is the cost associated with replacing the original asset. Generally used for such items as railroad ties and cross-arms for utility poles. Contrast with **retirement method of depreciation.**

report form. A vertical balance sheet presentation in which assets are shown at the top, followed by liabilities, and then owners' equity. contrast with **account form.**

representation letter. A letter from top management of a firm to the external auditors confirming certain matters of interest concerning the firm's financial activities. For example, the nature of any outstanding but unrecorded contingencies.

required rate of return. The minimum acceptable rate of return for the commitment of investment funds.

research & development costs. Expenditures made for investigation, prototype production, evaluation, and similar activities associated with the creation of new products. These costs are expensed when incurred unless incurred under contractual arrangement to develop products for others.

reserve. An outdated term related to such accounts as accumulated depreciation (reserve for depreciation), allowance for doubtful accounts (reserve for bad debts), etc. Currently should only refer to an appropriation of retained earnings.

reserve for encumbrances. In governmental accounting, the account that identifies that portion of the fund balance that has been committed. For example, travel claims, contracts, etc.

residual income. 1) Income accruing to common shareholders after preferred dividends. 2) The income that an investment center is able to earn above that specified by a given rate of return on assets.

residual value. The expected value of an asset at the end of its useful life.

responsibility accounting. The system of accounting whereby costs and revenues are collected and reported at the organization level having responsibility for their occurrence. The purpose is to assign individual managers responsibility for certain revenues and costs.

responsibility center. A cost, profit, or investment center in which the manager is held accountable for the activities of the center.

restatement. Revising an earlier financial statement due to a significant change in one or more items of data.

restrictive covenant. See **covenant.**

restricted retained earnings. See **appropriation of retained earnings.**

retail inventory method. A method of estimating ending inventory cost without taking physical stock. A ratio of cost to retail price is calculated and applied to sales in order to determine the cost of inventory sold.

retained earnings. The amount of income reinvested in a corporation and not distributed to stockholders in the form of dividends.

retained earnings statement. The financial statement that reflects the accumulated net income of a corporation less distributions to stockholders and transfers to contributed capital since inception of the firm or a quasi reorganization.

retirement. 1) The physical disposal of a fixed asset and removal of its cost and associated accumulated depreciation from the ledger. 2) Repurchase and cancellation of bonds payable, preferred stock, or common stock accompanied by the removal of their book values from the ledger.

retirement method of depreciation. A method of depreciation in which depreciation expense is only recognized when the asset is retired from service. The amount of the depreciation expense recognized is the original cost of the asset. Generally used for such items as railroad ties and cross-arms on utility poles. Contrast with **replacement method of depreciation.**

return on common stockholders' equity. See **ratios.**

return on total assets. See **ratios.**

revenue. The inflow of resources during a period as a result of providing goods or services.

revenue bond. A long-term debt security issued by a governmental authority in which periodic interest and maturity value are paid from earnings from an enterprise (such as city-owned water utility) owned by the governmental entity.

revenue expenditure. An outlay that is considered to benefit only the period in which it is incurred. The expenditure is charged to current operations and appears on the period's income statement as an expense. Contrast with **capital expenditure.**

revenue rulings. An instrument of the national office of the Internal Revenue Service to give an official interpretation of the tax law as it applies to a specific transaction.

reverse split. An exchange of a smaller number of new shares of stock for all of the existing shares. The effect of a reverse split is to increase the value of a share of stock while leaving each shareholder's relative position unchanged.

reversing entry. A journal entry made at the beginning of a period to eliminate the effect of an accrual adjusting entry so that certain transactions can be recorded in a standard and consistent manner.

review. A service offered by a CPA in which certain examination procedures are conducted to the extent that the CPA can make the statement that he is not aware of any material modifications that should be made to the financial statements in order for them to be in conformity with generally accepted accounting principles. The examination procedures are not made in accordance with generally accepted auditing standards.

revolving credit agreement. An agreement that obligates a financial institution to permit cumulative borrowing up to a specified limit. Since the lender is committed to make the funds available, a fee is normally charged on any unused portion of the credit limit.

rework. The repair of defective items on a manufacturing process.

right. A certificate giving the owner the option of purchasing a specified number (or fraction) of new shares of stock at a predetermined price. Rights are issued to existing stockholders on the basis of one right for each share owned.

rights-off. See **ex-rights.**

rights offering. The issue of rights to existing stockholders as a step in selling a new issue of securities. The rights may be used by stockholders to buy shares of stock at the subscription price or they may be sold to other investors.

rights-on. See **cum rights.**

risk premium. The portion of the rate of return required on an investment that is over and above the rate on a risk-free investment. The premium is compensation for the variability of an asset's return.

ROE. See **return on total assets** under **ratios.**

ROI. Return on investment.

royalty. Compensation for the right to use property such as a mine, book, or patent.

rulings. See **revenue rulings.**

S

safe harbor. The concept that authoritative bodies can or will provide guidelines to be followed in meeting the intent of some new tax or accounting procedure or requirement where precedent cases have not yet been established.

safety stock. The minimum amount of inventory required to provide for higher than expected demand and/or slow delivery of reordered items.

sale and leaseback. A leasing arrangement in which an organization sells an existing asset to another party who, in turn, leases it back to the seller.

sales. A revenue account showing the dollar amount of resources received for the delivery of a good or the providing of a service.

sales discounts. An account showing the reduction in the selling price of an item due to customers making payment within a certain period of time. Shown on the income statement as a reduction in gross sales.

sales journal. See **journals.**

sales mix. The relative proportion of each of a firm's products to total sales for the firm.

sales mix variance. See **variance.**

sales return and allowances. An account showing reductions in the invoice sales price of items due to returns or of reductions in original sales price because of defects.

sales tax. A tax based on a percentage of the selling price of an item.

sales-type lease. See **leases.**

sales volume variance. See **variance.**

salvage value. See **residual value.**

sample. A part of a population that is representative of the population as a whole.

sampling. A process of making judgments about a large group of items (the population) based on examination of a lesser number of items (the sample) chosen from the large group. See also **statistical sampling.**

sampling error. The difference in value between a sample and the population from which the sample is drawn. The larger a sample in relation to the population, the smaller the sampling error.

SAP. See **Statement on Auditing Procedures.**

SAS. See **Statement on Auditing Standards.**

schedule. Any form, worksheet, or report that is used for presenting or analyzing information. See also **spread sheet.**

scope. See **scope limitation.**

scope limitation. The restriction of the breadth of responsibility accepted by an auditor while performing an audit. Scope limitations are not desirable as they restrict the auditor's ability to perform those procedures necessary to express an opinion.

S corporation. A firm operating under the guidelines of Subchapter S of the Internal Revenue Code subsequent to the Subchapter S Revision Act of 1982.

scrap value. See **residual value.**

scrip dividend. See **dividend.**

SEC. See **Securities and Exchange Commission.**

secured bond. A long-term debt security that is backed as to interest and principal by having a claim on assets. See also **mortgage bond** and **collateral trust bond.**

Securities Act of 1934. A federal law that created the Securities and Exchange Commission. It provides for the registration of securities (beyond the initial offering) as well as the filing of annual and other periodic reports for companies traded on the major exchanges and over the counter (when assets exceed $3 million and the number of stockholders exceed 5001).

Securities Act of 1933. A federal law that sets forth the requirement that the initial offerings and distributions of certain securities must be registered.

Securities and Exchange Commission. A federal agency established in 1934 to regulate the listing, trading, and disclosure of public information of publicly traded securities.

security. A financial instrument that represents ownership, debt, or the right to buy or sell another financial instrument. Also see **collateral.**

segment. Any activity or part of an organization, such as a division, department, or product line, for which separate revenues and costs are accumulated and recorded.

segment margin. The excess of revenue over expenses directly associated and traceable to a segment.

segment reporting. Presentation of financial and other information by segments rather than for the entire organization. For example, reporting sales by line of product or division.

self insurance. The practice of internally providing for the possibility of losses as opposed to buying protection through transferring the risk to an insurance company.

self-liquidating loan. Debt incurred in acquiring current assets that, in turn, are sold for cash to repay the debt.

selling expense. Expenditures incurred in the promotion, marketing, and distribution of a product. For example, advertising and sales commissions.

semivariable costs. See **mixed costs.**

senior securities. Securities having claims that must be satisfied before any payments may be made to securityholders of lessor priority.

sensitivity analysis. The concept of applying "what if" situations to the assumptions used in researching a problem in order to determine if the conclusions drawn are still valid.

separate entity concept. The idea that the resources, liabilities, revenues, expenses, and other financial aspects of an economic activity should be accounted for apart from the activities of the owners.

serial bonds. Debt securities of a single issue that mature on sequential dates rather than all at one time. States, municipalities, and political subdivisions are major issuers of these obligations.

service life. The period of time over which an asset is expected to provide economic utility.

settlement date. The date on which the cash payment is due on securities that have been purchased or sold. The settlement date is five business days after the transaction date.

SFAC. See **statement of financial accounting concepts.**

SFAS. See **statement of financial accounting standards.**

share. A measure of ownership interest in a corporation. Also see **stock.**

shareholder. See **stockholder.**

short-term capital gain. The excess of sales price over adjusted cost or other basis of a capital asset. Not subject to special lower capital gains tax rate.

short-term capital loss. The excess of cost or other basis over sales price of a capital asset. Within limits a short-term capital loss may be used to reduce ordinary income.

short-term debt. Debt obligations that must be paid within one year.

shrinkage. Decline in inventory due to evaporation, melting, etc.

shutdown costs. Periodic expenses that will continue to be incurred even after an activity has stopped. Prior to the period of shutdown the expenses would have some other classification.

sight draft. A written order for immediate payment of a specific sum of money upon presentation.

significant variance. The difference between actual performance and budget that is large enough to warrant further investigation. See also **variance.**

simulation. A means of analyzing a problem whereby a model of reality is subjected to a series of random but logical assumptions in an effort to arrive a viable solution.

single-entry bookkeeping. A simple record keeping system in which transactions are noted in a single record such as a checkbook. Journals and ledgers are not maintained and financial statements can not be prepared directly from the records that are maintained.

sinking fund. Resources accumulated over time to provide for such eventualities as retirement of debt and replacement of operating assets.

S & L. Savings and loan.

social impact statement. A report of the positive (social benefits) and negative (social costs) impacts of a company's operations on society. For example, progress in hiring the handicapped and/or damage to the environment.

solvent. The ability to pay debts as they become due.

SOP. See **statement of position.**

source and use of funds statement. See **statement of changes in financial position.**

source and use of net working capital statement. See **statement of changes in financial position.**

source document. A document, such as a sales invoice, that is the basis for the information in a journal entry.

special journal. See **journals.**

specific identification. A method of determining the cost of inventory items sold. With this method a unique item is identified as the item exiting the inventory by means of a serial number or other unique characteristic.

spinoff. The payment of dividends consisting of securities of another corporation owned by the distributing firm.

split-off point. The point in a process at which individual activities no longer share in common costs also associated with other inseparable activities. Beyond split-off each activity incurs its own identifiable costs. See also **joint costs** and **joint products.**

spoilage. The loss of inventory due to causes such as rot and deterioration as well as failure to meet an acceptable quality standard.

spread sheet. A multicolumned schedule or worksheet used to accumulate, analyze, or present information. For example, a schedule reflecting, by month, the number of various items purchased.

standard costs. Predetermined costs that should be attained given reasonable deligence. Usually expressed on a per unit basis, these costs serve as a reasonable objective in an efficient organization as well as a point of departure for the evaluation of performance.

standard cost system. A method of accumulating costs in which deviations from predetermined standards are identified for analysis, control, and performance improvement. The procedure includes establishing the standard costs, comparing them to actual, and investigating the variances. Also see **variance.**

standard deduction. An outdated term for zero bracket amount.

standard deviation. In statistical analysis, a measure of the amount of variation associated with the expected value of a set of data.

standard labor rate. In a standard cost system, the wage rate established for a particular group of workers. See also **standard cost system.**

standard material rate. In a standard cost system, the predetermined unit cost of an item of raw material. See also **standard cost**

system.

stated value. A nominal value assigned to a security. See also **par value.**

statement. A formal presentation.

statement analysis. See **ratio analysis.**

statement of cash receipts and disbursements. See **statement of changes in financial position.**

statement of changes in financial position. The financial statement that reflects the sources and uses of funds for a period of time. This statement may be prepared on the basis of funds being defined as cash, cash plus marketable securities, or working capital. See also **total financial resources.**

statement of financial position. See **balance sheet.**

statement of position. Pronouncements issued by the Accounting Standards Division of the AICPA that set forth the practices and procedures of accounting for a particular type of economic activity whose accounting framework does not fit that of a normal concern. For example, Statement of Position 74-8 deals with accounting and reporting for colleges and universities. Traditionally, these pronouncements have been issued to fill a void until more authoritative guidelines are issued by the FASB or another appropriate body.

Statements on Auditing Procedures. The 54 pronouncements issued by AICPA's Committee on Auditing Procedure from 1939 to 1973 that set forth detailed acts to be followed by CPAs in conducting audits. Since 1973 similar pronouncements have been termed Statements on Auditing Standards.

Statements on Auditing Standards. Pronouncements issued by the AICPA's Auditing Standards Executive Committee (formerly Committee on Auditing Procedure) since 1973 that set forth detailed acts to be followed by CPAs in conducting audits. Prior to 1973 similar pronouncements were known as Statements on Auditing Procedures.

Statements of Financial Accounting Concepts. Pronouncements of the FASB dealing with the underlying fundamental procedures, practices, and theories of accounting.

Statements of Financial Accounting Standards. Final pronouncements of the Financial Accounting Standards Board that establish generally accepted accounting principles concerning certain aspects of financial accounting.

statistical sampling. A sampling technique that permits the user to quantitatively determine how reliable inferences drawn from a sample are likely to be as well as determine the risks associated with accepting the results. Statistical sampling methods commonly utilized in accounting include:

> **discovery sampling.** A sampling plan which provides an assurance of finding at least one deviation from the normal, if a significant number of deviations exists.
>
> **random sample.** A sampling technique in which all items in the large group have an equal chance of being selected.
>
> **sampling for attributes.** A sampling technique to estimate the rate of occurrence of some attribute in a large group.
>
> **sampling for variables.** A sampling technique to estimate the value of a specified variable for a large group of items.

statutory depletion. See **depletion.**

step cost. A cost that changes abruptly at certain levels of activity because it cannot be incurred in exact proportion to the activity that causes it. For example, if one supervisor can manage one to six employees, then another supervisor must be hired (with a large jump in supervisory costs) if seven employees are working.

stock. 1) Securities representing ownership in a corporation. 2) Items of inventory.

stock dividend. See **dividend.**

stockholder. One who is an owner of shares of a corporation.

stockholders' equity. The stockholders' claim to the assets of a firm after creditors' obligations have been met. Stockholders' equity is equal to assets minus liabilities or the sum of all stock accounts plus retained earnings.

stockholders' equity ratio. See **ratio.**

stock option. The right to purchase stock of a corporation for a specific price and within a prescribed time.

stock repurchase. Buying back shares of stock that have already been issued. The repurchased shares become treasury stock.

stock right. See **stock option.**

stock split. Sending stockholders additional shares and/or fractional shares for each share owned. Most stock splits are designed to reduce the stock price and no accounting adjustment to retained earnings takes place. A two for one split means an additional share is issued for each share already owned.

stock subscription. A pledge to buy stock of a corporation with payment to be made at a later date (usually in installments).

stock warrant. See **warrant.**

straight-line depreciation. A method of depreciation that allocates to each period a constant portion of an asset's original cost.

Subchapter S. A section of the Internal Revenue Code which permits a corporation of 35 or fewer stockholders (individuals or qualifying trusts) to elect that its earnings be taxed as if it were a partnership or proprietorship.

Subchapter S corporation. A firm operating under the guidelines of Subchapter S of the Internal Revenue Code prior to the Subchapter S Revision Act of 1982.

sublease. A lease agreement between a lessee and another party.

subordinated debt. Debt with a claim on income and assets that is of a lower priority than that of other securities which are outstanding.

subsequent events. Transactions or activities that occur after the date of the financial statements. If such events are material and occur prior to the issuance of the statements then they should be included in the statements.

subsidiary. A corporation that is controlled by another (parent) company. The parent owns over 50% of the subsidiary's outstanding voting stock.

subsidiary account. An account containing detailed information about one control account in the general ledger. For example, the accounts receivable subsidiary account would show individual customers and their balances, while the control account "accounts receivable" in the general ledger would show only the total of all accounts receivable.

subsidiary ledger. The book containing the accounts in which transactions associated with specific customers or creditors are recorded. See also **subsidiary account.**

substantive tests. Examinations made during an audit of financial statements in order to provide evidence as to whether reported account balances are proper.

sum-of-the-years'-digits method of depreciation. A method of accelerated depreciation in which a diminishing fraction of the long lived asset's cost less salvage is periodically recognized as an expense. The changing rate is determined by a numerator representing the years remaining in the asset's service life and the denominator is the sum of the number of years of expected economic life. For example in the second year of an asset with an expected 5-year life, the numerator would be 4 and the denominator would be 15.

sunk cost. An expenditure that has already been incurred and cannot be changed by any present or future decision so that it is irrelevant in analyzing future courses of action.

surplus. An outdated term for retained earnings

or earned surplus.

surtax. An additional tax based upon an already existing tax liability. A surtax is normally of a temporary nature.

suspense account. An account used to temporarily record data until a decision is made concerning the ultimate account to be used.

SYD. See **sum-of-the-years digits method of depreciation.**

T

T account. A synonym for an account in the ledger. So called because the account format resembles a capital T. Debits are shown under the left arm and credits under the right arm.

takeover. The purchase of one company by another when management of the acquired firm is opposed to the combination.

tangible asset. An asset that has physical substance, a life longer than one year, and is not in the ordinary course of business held for resale. See also **plant, property, and equipment.**

tariff. 1) A schedule of rates or fares. 2) A tax on imported goods.

taxable income. 1) Income subject to tax by a taxing authority. 2) That figure, total income less allowable deductions, which is used to calculate the tax liability.

tax allocation. See **interperiod tax allocation** and **intraperiod tax allocation.**

tax anticipation bill. Short-term securities issued by the U.S. Treasury that mature a week after quarterly corporate tax payment dates and that can be used at face value in payment of taxes.

tax avoidance. The minimizing of tax liability through legal techniques. The objective of effective tax planning. Contrast with **tax**

evasion.

tax benefit rule. A federal tax rule that provides tax relief in that it limits the recognition of income from the recovery of an expense or loss deducted in a prior year to the amount of the deduction that generated a tax benefit. For example, if one is limited by the formula for determining medical deductions to $500 in one year and the next year an insurance company reimburses him $700 for those expenses, only $500 should be claimed as income.

Tax Court. One of the three courts of original jurisdiction that decides cases concerning federal income, death and gift taxes.

tax credit. A dollar for dollar reduction in an income tax liability allowed by the Internal Revenue Code for some action. See also **investment tax credit.**

tax evasion. The elimination or reduction of taxes through subterfuge or fraud. Contrast with **tax avoidance.**

tax-free merger. A business combination that leaves the tax status of the firms and their securityholders unchanged.

tax option corporation. See **Subchapter S.**

tax preference item. Transactions receiving preferential treatment, that is, reduce taxable income, in determining the federal income tax liability. The most notable example is the use of an accelerated depreciation method resulting in a lower taxable income than would the use of a straight-line depreciation method.

tax shelter. An investment activity that results in unusual and beneficial treatment under the Internal Revenue Code so as to temporarily or permanently protect or defer a portion of income from current taxation. So called because the activity protects (shelters) income from ordinary tax treatment.

tax year. The period of time used by a taxpayer in determining a tax liability for federal tax purposes. Taxpayers must use the calender year unless another fiscal period is chosen.

128

T bill. See **Treasury bill.**

temporary account. An account that is used to collect or summarize accounting data before they are moved to another account. Temporary accounts have a zero balance at the end of an accounting period.

temporary investments. See **marketable securities.**

tenancy by the entirety. Joint ownership of an asset with the restriction that one co-owner may not sell or give away his or her interest without the consent of the other owner. This type of ownership is permitted only between married couples. See also **joint tenancy with right of survivorship** and **tenancy in common.**

tenancy in common. Joint ownership of an asset with the share of a deceased co-owner passing to heirs rather than to the other owner(s). See also **joint tenancy with right of survivorship** and **tenancy by the entirety.**

tender offer. A direct offer to shareholders to purchase all or part of their holdings of a specific stock at a specified price during a given period of time.

10-K. The financial report that must be filed annually with the Securities and Exchange Commission by companies with securities that are traded on a national exchange or in the over-the-market. The report contains complete audited statements and is available to the public for inspection.

10-Q. A quarterly report (usually unaudited) filed with Securities and Exchange Commission.

term bond. A long-term debt security that matures on a single, specified date. Contrast with **serial bond.**

term loan. A loan with a maturity of over one year and a specified schedule of repayment.

test of compliance. See **auditing.**

tick marks. Symbols, such as check marks and asterisks, used in auditing or other examinations to indicate that certain functions have been performed.

timing difference. The situation that arises when items of revenue or expense are included in the determination of accounting income in one period and in the determination of taxable income in another period. Recognition for accounting purposes may preceed or follow recognition for tax purposes. Over a sufficiently long enough period of time recognition will be the same under both accounting and tax purposes. Contrast with **permanent difference.**

total financial resources. The concept of funds that includes not only the sources and uses of cash or working capital but also includes any transaction that is considered simultaneously a source and use. An example would be giving stock to acquire a building.

trade acceptance. A written demand for payment of a specific sum of money on a future date by a seller of goods that is sent to and has been approved by the buyer of the goods.

trade credit. Accounts payable and accounts receivable originating from goods and services that have been received but not yet paid.

trade discount. The reduction in the retail price of an item when sold by a manufacturer or wholesaler to a retailer.

trading on the equity. Using the presence of stockholders' equity to borrow funds that can be invested at a rate in excess of the borrowing rate.

transaction. An event that is given accounting treatment and thus ultimately is reflected in the financial statements.

transaction cycle. A group of events that arise from related activities and move through progressive steps to the ultimate presentation on the financial statements. For example, the purchase cycle begins with the request for an item, progresses through the acquisition of the item, the payment of cash or recognition of a liability, and finally to the financial statements as an asset and expense with perhaps a corresponding liability.

transaction file. A file containing the temporary records associated with a specific transaction.

transfer agent. An organization, external to a corporation, that maintains the record of stock ownership for voting and dividend purposes.

transfer price. The exchange amount at which goods are moved from one segment of a business to another. For example, the price charged by a paper producing segment to a bag producing segment of the same organization. Essentially, an internal sales price.

translation exposure. The exposure to potential shifts in income and net worth due to having assets in foreign countries subject to revaluations because of variations in exchange rates.

treasurer. The officer in a corporation who is responsible for cash management and investments.

Treasury bill. A short-term debt security issued by the U.S. Treasury at a discount from face value. Also called a T bill.

treasury bond. 1) A long-term debt security that was previously issued and outstanding but was required either by purchase, gift, or settlement of debt and not retired. Periodic interest is not paid. 2) A long-term debt issue of the U.S. Treasury. Unlike Treasury bills that are sold at a discount and pay no explicit interest, Treasury bonds make semi-annual interest payments.

Treasury note. An intermediate-term debt security issued by the U.S. Treasury.

treasury stock. Shares of a firm's stock that have been issued and then repurchased and held in its treasury. The repurchase may occur because the shares are needed for some specific purpose (stock options or merger) or simply due to the firm having extra funds available at a time when investment alternatives seem unattractive.

trial balance. A list of the accounts with their

balances appearing in a ledger. The total debits should equal the total credits. A trial balance is usually prepared at the end of a period and is considered the first step in preparing financial statements.

troubled debt restructuring. A change in the terms of an obligation in which the lender grants some concession(s) to the borrower that the former would not normally consider. The concessions may take various forms such as lengthening the payment period or accepting a smaller payment than is legally due.

trust. An arrangement whereby one party (the trustee) takes title to property owned by another party (the grantor) for the purpose of protecting or conserving the property for either the grantor or a third party (beneficiary). The grantor establishes the trust.

trustee. 1) A third party (generally a commercial bank) who looks out for the interests of bondholders under the terms of a bond indenture. 2) A court-appointed official in a bankruptcy proceeding whose job it is to develop a plan for reorganization and oversee the bankrupt firm's assets. 3) The conserver of assets in a trust.

trust fund. The resources or property held by a trustee of a trust.

trust receipt. A written document in which a borrower acknowledges receipt of certain physical inventory with title remaining in the name of the lender. When proceeds from a sale are forwarded to the lender, title is released. Floor planning by automobile dealers utilizes trust receipts.

turnover. The frequency with which an asset is turned into sales. Examples include fixed asset turnover, inventory turnover, and receivables turnover. Also see **ratios.**

U

UCC. See **Uniform Commercial Code.**

unamortized bond discount. That portion of the bond discount that has not yet been written off by increasing the periodic interest expense. Unamortized bond discount is subtracted from the par or maturity value to arrive at the book value of the bonds shown on the balance sheet.

unamortized bond premium. That portion of the bond premium that has not yet been written off by decreasing the periodic interest expense. Unamortized bond premium is added to the par or maturity value to arrive at the book value of the bonds shown on the balance sheet.

unappropriated retained earnings. Earnings not restricted and available for the declaration of dividends.

unaudited statements. Financial statements that have not been examined for presentation in accordance with generally accepted accounting principles.

unavoidable costs. See **sunk costs.**

uncollectible account. An account receivable or note receivable that was not paid when due and which all evidence indicates will not be paid in the future.

unconsolidated subsidiary. A subsidiary that is not included in the group of companies comprising a set of consolidated financial statements because it is a foreign company, has a completely different type of operation from the other companies in the group, or has a financial structure that is not comparable with the group.

uncontrollable costs. Costs that cannot be controlled at a given level of management or within a certain time period.

underapplied overhead. The excess of actual manufacturing overhead incurred for a period over manufacturing overhead applied to production.

underwrite. The purchase of a security issue by an investment banker for resale at a higher price.

undistributed profit. 1) Profit of a partnership, S corporation, or other business venture that has not yet been allocated to the appropriate parties. 2) Profit of a partnership, S corporation, or other similar type of business that has been assigned to a particular individual but no payment out of the firm has been made. Similar to retained earnings of a corporation.

undivided profit. See **undistributed profit.**

unearned revenue. The Inflow of assets received in advance of providing a good or service, such as receipt of payment for a magazine subscription, that will be delivered over a number of months or years. Unearned revenues are shown as a liability until they are earned by providing the goods or services.

unfunded pension plan. A pension plan under control of the company instead of an independent agency. Benefits to retired employees are made by the company.

Uniform Commercial Code. Statutes on various business subjects that were drafted and then adopted by most of the states in order to secure some degree of uniformity in handling business transactions in the United states.

unissued stock. Stock that has been authorized but that has not yet been issued.

134

unlimited liability. A characteristic of the noncorporate form of business in which the owner(s) may be personally responsible for payment of obligations associated with the business. So called because an owner's loss is not limited to his investment.

unpaid dividends. 1) Dividends that have been declared but have not yet been paid. 2) Dividends on cumulative preferred stock that have been passed.

unqualified opinion. An audit opinion issued by a certified public accountant stating that the financial statements give a fair presentation of what they purport to show in accordance with generally accepted accounting principles.

unrealized gain. An increase in the value of an asset held and not sold. Unrealized gains are not generally recognized in accounting records.

unrealized increment. A rare and unique situation that results in the write-up of an asset. Such write-ups are not shown on the income statement but rather are reflected as an increase in the owners' equity section of the balance sheet.

unrealized loss. A decrease in the value of an asset held and not sold. If the loss is considered to be other than temporary it is recognized as a loss on the income statement.

unsecured bond. See **debenture.**

unsecured loan. A loan which is backed by the borrower's promise of repayment but not by specific assets.

useful life. The period of time over which an asset is expected to provide an economic benefit.

V

validate. To certify or test for accuracy.

validity test. In auditing, an analysis to determine if an item is accurate.

valuation account. A contra account used to offset another account.

value. The worth of an item expressed in terms of money.

value-added tax. A tax on the increase in worth of a product at each level of production or distribution. The tax is paid in the form of a higher retail price by the ultimate consumer. This type of tax is used in some foreign countries, particularly those in the European Common Market.

variable costing. The method of accounting for manufacturing cost in which only variable costs (direct material, direct labor, and variable manufacturing overhead) are treated as product costs and all other costs are treated as period costs. Contrast with **absorption costing.**

variable costs. Expenditures that vary, in the aggregate, in direct proportion to changes in the level of activity that causes the expenditures. The emphasis is on total dollar amount. That is, the total cost rises and falls as the activity level rises and falls, but the cost per unit of activity remains constant.

variable overhead. Manufacturing overhead that varies in total with the level of production but on a per unit basis remains constant.

variable overhead efficiency variance. See **variance.**

variable overhead spending variance. See **variance.**

variable rate loan. A debt obligation that carries an interest rate pegged to some predetermined formula. As a result, interest on the loan may be altered at specified intervals.

variance. The difference between an actual result and the expected, budgeted, or standard result. Variance analysis is frequently utilized in standard cost systems. Variances commonly used in variance analysis include:

> **budget variance.** The difference between the amount budgeted and actual results. Also called overhead spending variance.

> **capacity variance.** See **production volume variance.**

> **direct labor efficiency variance.** The standard labor rate times the difference between the actual direct labor hours used in production and the standard direct labor hours allowed.

> **direct labor rate variance.** The difference between the actual and standard wage rates times the number of actual hours used in production.

> **direct labor variance.** The algebraic sum of direct labor efficiency variance and direct labor rate variance.

> **direct materials price variance.** The difference between actual prices paid for materials purchased and a predetermined price standard. It may also be calculated on the basis of materials put into production rather than purchased.

> **direct materials quantity variance.** The standard unit price times the difference between the actual quantity of materials

137

used in production and standard quantities allowed for the number of units produced.

direct materials variance. The algebraic sum of the direct materials price variance and the direct materials quantity variance.

fixed overhead spending variance. The difference between actual fixed overhead and budgeted fixed overhead.

idle capacity variance. See **production volume variance.**

overhead volume variance. See **production volume variance.**

production volume variance. Budgeted fixed overhead less applied fixed overhead. This variance is the result of operating at a volume level other than the one used to establish the fixed overhead rate. Also called capacity variance, volume variance, and idle capacity variance.

sales mix variance. The difference between actual and forecasted sales mix. The difference is due to a change in sale patterns associated with products having different profit ratios.

sales volume variance. The difference between actual and forecasted sales as a result of changes in volume (as opposed to a change in price).

variable overhead efficiency variance. The difference between actual direct labor hours and standard direct labor hours times the standard variable overhead rate per direct labor hour. This definition is based on the use of direct labor hours as the basis for allocating variable overhead. Alternative bases, such as machine hours, may also be used.

variable overhead spending variance. The difference between actual variable overhead and the variable overhead rate times actual direct labor hours. If direct labor hours are not used as the basis for allocating variable overhead then some other appropriate basis, such as machine hours, may be used.

volume variance. See **production volume variance.**

variance analysis. In a standard cost system, the study of the differences between predetermined standard costs and actual costs. The primary objective of this type of analysis is to determine and explain the causes of the variances. The difference is considered favorable if actual costs are less than standard costs and unfavorable if actual costs exceed standard costs. See also **variance.**

VAT. See **value-added tax.**

verifiable. The concept that information is determined and presented in such an objective manner that similar results could be obtained by an equally qualified individual working independently.

vertical merger. A combination of two or more firms which are involved in different stages of production of the same general product.

vested benefits. Pension benefits earned by an employee that are not contingent upon the employee continuing in the service of the employer.

vesting. The rights to retirement benefits made possible by contributions from an individual's employer.

volume discount. A reduction in selling price due to ordering a minimum number of units or dollars worth of merchandise during a stipulated time period.

volume variance. See **variance.**

voucher. A form serving as evidence of cash disbursements that is utilized to establish control over expenditures.

voucher payable. An account used in place of accounts payable (especially in governmental accounting) when vouchers are utilized.

vouching. The auditing procedure of tracing a transaction back to its documentary support.

W

warehouse receipt. A written document acknowledging that specified goods are being stored in a warehouse.

warrant. An option to purchase a given number of shares of a firm's common stock at a specified price per share until a certain date. Warrants are often included as part of a new bond issue in order to reduce interest costs on the bonds.

warranty. A guarantee that a good or service will perform as intended for a stated period of time or that the defect will be corrected at no additional expense to the purchaser.

warranty cost. The cost to the seller of providing a warranty.

wash sale. The sale of a security at a loss when a substantially identical security has been purchased within 30 days of the sale. Wash sales are legal but the loss cannot be used as a deduction from gross income for tax purposes.

waste. Residue from a manufacturing process that essentially has no value. Contrast with **by-product** and **joint product.**

wasting asset. Natural resources such as coal and oil that are consumed during use. Also applied to items such as timber which can be replaced. See also **depletion.**

watered stock. Capital stock in an entity with overvalued assets.

W-4 form. A statement filed by an employee with his employer indicating the number of exemptions being claimed for tax purposes. The employer uses this information to determine the income tax withholding.

when issued. Trading in a security prior to the date it is actually issued.

windfall. An unexpected gain.

window dressing. The act of making financial statements more appealing by overstating income or assets and understating expenses or liabilities. For example, failure to recognize that all accounts receivable will not be collected via the use of an allowance for uncollectible accounts is a form of window dressing.

withholding taxes. The amount of funds deducted from an employee's gross pay and paid to a tax authority by his or her employer.

working capital. The excess of current assets over current liabilities. The term is also often used to refer to the dollar amount of a firm's current assets.

work-in-process inventory. Goods in a manufacturing process that have been started but have not been completed at the end of the accounting period.

workers' compensation. Cash payments and medical care for workers who are injured in the course of their employment. Benefits are paid regardless of who is at fault.

workpapers. An auditor's personal record of the work performed and conclusions reached during the process of auditing an entity.

writ. A legal document from a judge requiring that something be done.

writedown. A reduction in the balance of an account due to unusual circumstances. See also **writeoff.**

writeoff. The loss of value of an asset or a losing operation that is used to reduce income on a firm's financial statements. For example, the reduction in carrying value of inventory due to obsolence is "written off" by showing it as a reduction in the calculation of net income. See also **writedown**.

writeup. An increase in the book value of an asset. This is not considered a generally accepted accounting practice.

W-2 form. A statement issued by an employer to indicate an individual employee's earnings and taxes withheld from those earnings during the year. A copy is sent to the employee as well as to the appropriate tax authorities. Although the form is a federal form copies are also sent to state and local tax officials.

Y

year-end adjustment. A ledger account adjustment at the end of a fiscal year to account for an unusual or unrecorded transaction.

yield. The return received from an investment.

yield curve. The relationship between maturity and yield. A positively-sloped curve is produced by long-term securities carrying higher yields than short-term securities.

yield to maturity. The average annual yield on a bond if it is held until maturity. This measure of yield takes into account both annual interest payments and any increase or decrease in value which will occur between the purchase date and maturity date.

Z

ZBB. See **zero-base budgeting.**

zero-base budgeting. An approach to budgeting that requires that managers justify all budgetary programs each period. Traditional budgeting normally requires justification only for changes from preceding budget levels.

zero-bracket amount. A deduction generally available to all taxpayers in calculating personal taxable income. Replaces the older concept of a standard deduction. For 1979 and thereafter this amount is $2,300 for single individuals and head of households, $3,400 for married persons filing jointly, and $1,700 for married persons filing separately.

zero-coupon bond. A long-term debt security in which the issuer makes no semi-annual interest payments. The bonds are issued at significant discounts from face value and a holder's income results from the difference between the discounted price paid and the price received at the time of sale (face value if at maturity). Except for tax-free issues, holders of zero-coupon bonds must report and pay taxes on the implicit income received each year even though no actual interest payments are made.